"Your family is a snare of Satan."

Rachel's story is one in three million—the estimated three million American young people ensnared in some five thousand religious cults today. Many come from fine, loving homes. Most often, they first encounter the cult members during a period of anxiety and uncertainty, such as before and after exams or after a romantic breakup.

That's how Rachel was when she saw the two long-robed men.

ESCAPE tells of the oppressive life under "Brother Evangelist" Jim Roberts . . . of the total subjection of the women to the commands and teachings of the "brothers" . . . of how smiling or laughing was discouraged . . . of eating toss-away food from behind fast-food restaurants . . . of fleeing from city to city to avoid concerned families ("snares of Satan") . . . of Rachel's family and friends, who searched and prayed desperately for her until her rescue.

Escape

The True Story Of A Young Woman Caught In The Clutches Of A Religious Cult

Rachel Martin, dressed in the garb and backpack required for life in the cult. Photo by Dean Barron

£1.95

Escape

**RACHEL
MARTIN
AS TOLD TO
BONNIE PALMER YOUNG**

Pickering & Inglis
LONDON · GLASGOW

This book is dedicated to my friends, Nikki, Janet, Philip, Danny, Cathy, Allison, and all those who have experienced the clutches of the Jim Roberts cult. And to the many others who've been taken in by other cults.

My prayer for all of you is that you have found or will find the true path of life through Jesus Christ, in His Word, the Bible. It is only in knowing God in the way He really is, not as the cults say that He is, that you will find the reality, the meaning, the happiness, the purpose and fulfillment that we were all trying to find in the cults.

Rachel Martin Dugger

1
Just Like The Apostles

Without buying anything in the little suburban grocery store, I went back outside.

The early evening Nebraska heat slammed into me and I wiped my hand across my bronzed features, brushing away the perspiration. I kicked up the stand on my bike and would probably have ridden it back to the apartment, had I not seen two bearded young men across the street.

Kearney, Nebraska, is a college town but it has its roots in stolid, middle-class America. We usually didn't see long, flowing robes and sandals on men in our part of the country. Their robes were smudged with the grime of the road and even from where I stood, some distance away, I could see that their bearded faces were smeared and sooty, as though it had been a long while since they had washed. Yet, I was intrigued by their appearance.

Another weird, religious outfit, I told myself. *They're probably Hare Krishnas.* That was the only group I had learned anything about and I actually knew little of what they believed—only what people said about them. I wondered how far from the Bible they were.

I knew it was foolish of me to approach two complete strangers, and at night. But I was so distraught by events of the past few weeks that my usual caution and reserve had evaporated. Besides, I had been raised in a Christian home and a good church. I took pride in my knowledge of the Bible and what it taught. I thought it would be interesting to discuss religion with the two young men across the street. Perhaps I could even share Christ with them and show them how wrong they were. I could see myself in Sunday school class, sharing my experience of this night with the others. It gave me a feeling of righteousness—a dedicated, informed believer who could judge the spiritual condition and knowledge of others in a few brief moments.

Sauntering over to the solemn-faced young men in their dirty cassocks, I thought how much they looked the way the disciples of Christ must have looked. There was a holy air about them, an "other worldliness" that set them apart from anyone I had ever met before. In my mind I could see the two of them on the shores of the Sea of Galilee, their boats and nets abandoned on the beach behind them, as they followed Jesus.

One was tall and thin, his head shaved bare. The other was shorter, rather stocky in build, his tangled hair clipped short. The smell of their unwashed bodies and clothes was strong about them and I found myself wrinkling my nose distastefully. I was sure they noticed my reaction, but if they did, they did not respond to it. They smiled wanly and I found myself smiling in return.

I don't believe they would have spoken to me at all, had I not been the first to speak. But I approached boldly and asked what they were doing in a quiet little town like Kearney, Nebraska. They would not have seemed so out of place on the streets of Hollywood or in the airport at Denver.

They looked down at me, very much as one might in replying to a rather stupid question from a child. "We're just trying to be Christians like those in the New Testament," one of them said.

"And we're trying to tell others about Him, so they, too, can escape the wrath of God that is soon to be visited on this wicked world."

"That's neat," I replied. "I'm trying to be a Christian, too." I didn't let them know what a miserable job of it I was doing.

"The Lord has shown us that we have to come out from the world and be separate," one of them informed me. "We have to flee carnality and wickedness, holding ourselves above the temptations that are all around us."

I winced inwardly. Their words were a lance to my heart that left it bleeding.

"If you stay in the world," his companion went on, seriously, "you are going to get caught in all the activities and inventions of the world and forget about God. Look at the people who live in these houses." He gestured boldly at the homes on either side of the street. "What do the people who live here care about? New cars and color television and swimming pools in the back yard. They call themselves Christian, but they don't *really* care about God."

I had to admit that was true. If I were to be completely honest, I would have had to say that I didn't care about Him, either. Not really. If I did, I wouldn't be so concerned about my financial problems and what I could do with my life. I would turn everything to Him and trust Him to straighten out the mess I was in.

As we talked, my thoughts fled back to the events that had taken place earlier in the evening . . . I remember turning slowly, fumbling to get the phone back on its cradle. For some reason Jesus Christ's sad face came to mind, misty and blurred by my own hot tears. I had looked away, as though to avoid those all-knowing eyes.

And I called myself a Christian! Me, Rachel Martin. Liar and hypocrite. Yes, I was in church every Sunday, and I knew all the right answers to deceive the pastor and the members of the congregation. They could call on me to sing or pray or give a testimony and I could acquit myself commendably, but at night a new Rachel shed her cocoon of piety and flew with the world.

I was embraced by each set of friends and acquaintances as one of their own. Only I and a close inner circle of friends knew of my duplicity, and they wouldn't reveal my secret. Most of them were trying to do the same as I.

Trembling, I crossed the living room of the apartment my closest friend, Sue Delano, and I had rented a few days before, and stood before the window. The terrible guilt and self-loathing that had dominated my life the past few months gnawed at me, making me miserable. Sue had only recently placed her trust in Christ. What would she think if she knew the truth about me?

Phil had called again. I didn't know why. I thought we had ended our affair before I left for my vacation. We had decided that we were not going to see each other any more. But he had just phoned and wanted to take me out again. If I gave in and saw him, I knew how that date would end—the same way they had been ending for the past few months, in a wave of shame that would leave me even more dejected and miserable than before. I had determined that it was not going to happen again. When he called and I learned his purpose in phoning me, I had hung up. But I was shaken by the way my pulse raced when I heard his voice.

I knew Phil had already found other girl friends who would take my place if I persisted in my decision not to go out with him any more. I was torn by remorse and jealousy. I couldn't stand the thought of his putting his arms around someone else and whispering that he loved her. Even though I would know it to be a lie, I longed to hear him say once more that I was first in his life, that there had never been anyone before me. At the same time, I realized that our relationship could not go on. I had to break it off.

I looked down at the wide tree-lined street of this Nebraska town I had come to from Denver, Colorado after graduating from high school. A few weeks before, I would have been gripped by excitement about that same time in the evening. I would have been dressing for Phil to pick me up. And for one terrifying instant, I wondered if I was strong enough to keep my resolve not to go with him any more. At the moment I was afraid that if he drove up I would have flown to the car and gone off with him, pushing aside my resolve to clean up that area of my life. Bleakly, however, I realized that it was all over between Phil and me. I had been so firm with him that he would never phone me again. And without him, I had only an empty fall and winter before me.

Sue had come in from the bedroom just then and had seen the consternation on my face. She didn't know what was wrong, beyond the fact that Phil and I were having trouble. I couldn't bring myself to tell her.

"Are you all right?" she asked.

"I'm fine," I lied. "In fact, I've never been better."

But she knew me well enough to know I was not speaking the truth. "Do you want to go with Bill and me?" she asked. "I know he wouldn't mind."

A great weariness enveloped me as I went over and sat down. "I think I'd rather stay here. Maybe I'll get a chance to talk to Phil again and get this mess straightened out."

I see now that I hadn't really wanted to break off my affair with him any more than he wanted to stop seeing me, but at the time my emotions were in such a turmoil I was sure he was the only one who was trying to keep us together.

At the door Sue turned back, sensing my deep depression. "Are you sure you're all right?"

"Of course I am." I managed a thin smile. At that moment I was actually glad to have her go. I didn't feel like talking to anyone.

When I was finally alone in our bright new little apartment I went over and picked up my Bible. Mother and Dad had given it to me. How many years ago? The date was on the flyleaf but I could not bring myself to look at it right then. Just seeing Dad's familiar handwriting hurt too much. He had taught me to turn to the

Word of God when I was troubled or tempted to sin.

But he had never once suspected that I could ever drift so far from Christ. Something had happened to the little girl he had given that Bible to so long ago. Something ugly and unclean. I had been taught to live a better way than I was living. My parents, my church and the Christian school I had attended before our family moved to Denver two years earlier had all stressed separation from the world. How had I allowed myself to be caught in the web I now found myself in?

Uncertainly, I leafed through the Bible in my hand. I wanted to read it as I had so many times in the past, but there was no comfort in the Word for me that night. Its words seemed like a sword cutting through my heart. I laid it down quickly, as though it was suddenly too hot to hold, and left the apartment.

My stomach was a ball of ice and my head was pounding with tension. In recent weeks, as my problems multiplied, I had taken to eating compulsively. I wasn't hungry, yet I felt that food might, somehow, ease my frustration and pain. I was gaining weight, a fact I also found disturbing. It seemed that I couldn't do anything right.

I got on my bike and pedaled down the street to Bob's Quick Shop, the little suburban grocery where Sue and I had started doing most of our buying since moving into the neighborhood. The girl at the checkout stand spoke to me as I came in but I scarcely heard her. I paused, uncertain about taking a cart, then turned and hurried on.

Walking up and down the familiar aisles did little to quiet my heart. I was so distraught that even food failed to interest me. I was standing in front of the baked goods, wondering how many pounds chocolate covered doughnuts would put on, when a girl I used to work with spied me and came over.

"Rachel!" she exclaimed, "I didn't expect to see you here tonight."

I mumbled something unintelligible and would have moved away before she had an opportunity to continue the conversation, but Carole had a dress pattern to show me. "I got some material on sale today and I'm going to make this outfit. Isn't it darling?"

I wasn't much interested in her new dress right then, but I tried to act excited.

"I wish I had a piece of the material along to show you," she burbled. "It's really neat." Only then did she become aware of my preoccupation. "What *are* you doing here?" she demanded.

I knew what she was talking about, but pretended not to. "I'm trying to find something that looks good," I said, evasively. "But everything I think I would like is fattening."

"I know just what you mean." She turned to her shopping and I moved on, gratefully.

My affair with Phil was only part of my troubles. The last few months I had been increasingly disturbed with myself and my lot in life. Rather than go to Western Bible College in Denver where Dad was a printer, I had moved to Kearney and had taken a job with a local dentist. I thought being on my own and having money to spend the way I wanted to would be the answer, but I soon learned there was no satisfaction in that. My headaches and the pains in my stomach persisted. When the doctor could find nothing physically wrong with me he decided my problems stemmed from boredom and recommended a change of job and surroundings. I didn't tell him about my chameleon-like existence and the turmoil it was causing.

Each morning I had gone to work wearing the smiling guise of a happy, carefree receptionist—while I was miserable inside. I had been thinking about enrolling in the local beauty school. The doctor's suggestion for change was the only impetus I needed.

But, I decided, there was going to be more to it than that. I was going to break off my affair with Phil. I gave the dentist notice that I was quitting so I could go to beauty school, and applied for an evening waitress job. Only that day I had received a phone call telling me the job was mine. The way things were working out, I should have been happy.

I reasoned that I would have no more difficulties, if only Phil could be understanding and accept the fact that I would not go out with him anymore, and if I hadn't spent so much money on my recent vacation with Sue to visit my sister and her family in Washington, D.C. I had returned to Kearney with my beauty school fees paid and a meager four dollars in my purse.

My dad would have loaned me the money if I had gone to him, but I didn't want to do that. I would only be opening myself to a certain lecture about the will of God and living a separated life. I couldn't handle anything like that right then. No, this was something I had to work out for myself.

And now I had met the two long-robed young men who seemed so sincere about spending the rest of their lives telling people of their faith in Jesus Christ. We talked for a few minutes about what it meant to be a Christian and live a life pleasing to God. Their answers were quick and sure and, insofar as I was able to determine, as well based on the Scriptures as my own. At least they quoted a lot of Bible verses.

The strangers showed such deep interest in me that when they asked questions about my life I was eager to share with them. At last, I thought, here were some people who cared about me. I told them about my job as a dentist's receptionist, and that I had given notice so I could quit at the end of the week and go to beauty school. I thought they would be pleased to hear that, but they were disturbed by it.

"You shouldn't be working for a dentist or waiting tables in a cafe or doing anything else for money," they told me. "That is working for man and it is a sin for a

Christian. You should be spending all your time working for God."

I tried to argue with them. "But I need money to pay my bills," I protested. They had made their ideas sound so logical and Biblical that I felt guilty about having to work.

"If you really have the faith in God you say you have," they told me, "you should be able to step out and trust Him for all your needs. You wouldn't have to look to man for money to take care of yourself."

They went on to share their experiences with me, telling how God had taken care of them wherever they were, whatever they were doing, how He had provided all their food and clothing. One of them had needed a pair of shoes before leaving California on this trip. Humanly speaking, it had seemed foolish for him to start on such a journey without good shoes, but he knew God wanted him to go east, so he went. They hadn't traveled more than a few miles when he found a pair of shoes in good condition and in his exact size along the road. "God put them there just for me," he concluded.

By this time they seemed to realize I was getting interested. They didn't know that much of my interest was generated by the problems I faced. Perhaps God had allowed me to get into such a mess in order to prepare me for my visit with these two servants of His.

"The Bible tells us that many are called but few are chosen," they said. "How about you? Are you going to be one of those who hears, but the seed falls on stony ground, or are you going to forsake all and follow Jesus?"

I hesitated. What they said had the ring of truth, and they used the Bible to prove what they believed. That bothered me the most. I had always been taught that the cults would ignore or distort the Scriptures. I had even heard ministers say we should test what people said about the Bible to learn whether they are true believers or not. Now these men were saying the same thing. "See what the Bible has to say," they challenged me. "You'll find out that we're teaching truth and what you have heard at home and in church is in error."

If I had known as much about the Scriptures as I thought I did I probably would have seen the subtle way in which they were manipulating them, but I was not prepared for an approach like this. My intense new friends were so quick to quote Scripture for every situation that I was awed by their knowledge of the Bible. I thought they must be the final authorities on anything Scriptural.

"You claim to be a Christian," they continued, "but you are talking about going to beauty school to help women make themselves more attractive so they can be a snare to men. '. . . Beauty is vain,' " they quoted from Proverbs 31:30, " 'but a woman that feareth the Lord, she shall be praised.' "

I was convinced that what they told me was true. Looking back, I don't see how I could have been so completely deceived, but in my bewilderment and confusion they offered me a way of escape. "What should I do to be like you?" I asked.

"Give up your association with the world and live the way God directs His people to live. Then you will be what He wants you to be."

I considered their confident directive briefly. In that moment I didn't think I had ever met anyone so firm in their convictions—anyone so sure they had all the right answers and knew exactly what God wanted them to do. "Do you think I should go with you?" I asked.

They were motionless, staring at me. When they spoke, they did not answer me directly. "Where do you live?" they wanted to know, speaking as though my decision had already been made.

"Eight or ten blocks from here." I gestured in the direction of the house where we had an apartment.

They started in that direction and I walked with them, wheeling my bike. Without their asking or my consenting, we were on the way to the place I lived to get some of my things.

I began to think about Dr. Prellwitz, the dentist I worked for. He had been so good to me while I worked there, and so understanding when I gave him notice that I wanted to quit. I didn't want to cause him any trouble, and if I didn't show up at my desk the following morning I would make it hard for him. He wouldn't have a new receptionist until the following Monday.

"I agreed to stay with the dentist until Saturday afternoon," I told the two men. "Maybe I should do that and join you later."

I read the disapproval on their faces. "Do you have a contract?" they wanted to know.

"No, there was no written contract, but I had given him my word."

"Then you don't owe him anything. You can leave any time you wish."

We approached the broad, square, two-story house where Sue and I had so recently taken an apartment. It was a proud old building, erected in the days before college dormitories, when the people of the community had picked up a few extra dollars each month housing teachers in training. White wooden pillars guarded the porch and a great bay window looked out over the quiet street.

Sue and I had both fallen in love with the grand old house from the first moment we saw the *Apartment For Rent* sign in the window. We had pulled into the parking lot behind it and hurried to the door, fearful that someone else would get there ahead of us, or that we would find there was some mistake and the apartment was not for rent after all. But there was no error. The apartment was available and, amazingly, the rent was low enough for us to afford.

Now I was going back to this same apartment which had thrilled us so much only a few days before, to gather a few personal belongings and leave town with these new friends.

I would need my sewing things, they said, emptying the drawers of my machine into a grocery sack. Their group was large and the sisters had the responsibility of sewing and mending. Needles, thread and pins were important. I would also need my toothbrush, toothpaste, soap, towels and sleeping bag.

I glanced at the clothes I had placed out on the bed earlier—the outfit I had planned to wear to work the next day. I giggled impulsively.

"Is there something wrong, Sister?" they wanted to know.

"I just happened to notice the clothes I planned to wear to work in the morning," I said, giggling again.

"When God's appointed time comes," Brother Josiah, the older, blond one said seriously, "we have to respond—if we are to escape the wrath of God."

I sensed his disapproval.

"What about clothes?" I asked.

They went to my closet and inspected my dresses with critical eyes. Only the two new smocks I had made to wear to beauty school were godly enough to take, they informed me. The rest of my wardrobe would have to be left behind. I was disturbed by that, but challenged, too. Faith wasn't worth much unless it cost something. The very fact that I was going to have to give up my clothes made me feel good—almost clean. At last I was doing something worthwhile.

Even though I felt I was in the center of God's will in going with the two young strangers that night, I was slow in getting my things together. Sue had said she would be home early. Perhaps she would come back before I left. I suddenly wanted to talk to her, to learn what she thought about my new friends and the gospel they preached. If I could only tell her about the group and the way they depended on God for everything, she might be interested in going along, too. If she could add the faith of the brothers to her new life in Jesus Christ she would be living close to Him. And, having her along would be good for me, too. We could strengthen each other in the faith.

But she did not come and my companions were getting restive. They kept looking at the clock and watching the door, as though fearful she would return before we left.

"Hurry, Sister," they urged.

I looked around, my uncertainty growing. For a quick instant I wondered if I was doing the right thing. Then I thought of the disciples and the way they had left their nets and their boats to follow Jesus.

"Hurry," my new friends repeated.

That did it. "I think we have everything I'll need," I said.

One of the brothers stopped in the kitchen long enough to scoop up some food and take a few bowls.

"Do you have a car?" he asked at the foot of the stairs.

"I thought you said we shouldn't use cars," I replied, surprised by his question. "Aren't they the tools of Satan?"

"They are," Brother Josiah told me without hesitation, "and we won't keep it very long. We'll probably sell it in a few days, but perhaps the Lord will let us use it. If He will, it will make traveling much easier."

We went out to my parking place. The two robed men were just climbing into the back seat of my 1969 LeMans when Sue drove up, pulling into the space next to me. She was using more than the width alloted to her and laughingly mentioned the terrible angle at which she had parked. I sighed my relief, silently thanking God for her appearance. But the brothers seemed as upset as I was pleased.

"We'd better go, Sister," one of them murmured, little above a whisper.

Almost at the same instant, Sue noticed that I was not alone. She turned her flashlight on the brothers in the rear seat. I saw her flinch and knew that she was startled to see the strange, bearded men in my car. But she did not ask any questions.

"I'm leaving, Sue," I told her, trying to keep down the wild hammering of my heart. I wanted her to come over to the car and insist on knowing where I was going and urge me to stay with her, but she didn't. I'm sure she thought we were only leaving to drive around for a while and would be back soon. It was all so quiet and commonplace, like a hundred other dates I had had, that I had some difficulty in believing I was actually leaving Kearney with two strange men whom I had only known for an hour or so.

"Where are you going?" she asked, as I got into the car. I think she sensed, for the first time, that this was to be no ordinary drive.

As she spoke, the one called Brother Josiah leaned forward intently. I could tell by the sound of his voice that he was suddenly very agitated, as though something was about to happen that could upset their plans. "Sister," he whispered in my ear, "we have to leave. Don't talk to her any more. She may be a snare of Satan."

That hardly seemed possible to me. Sue was a Christian and one of my best friends. She wouldn't do anything that would lead me away from God. Besides, I really wanted to explain to her where I was going and why. She ought to have a chance to join us, too.

A few moments ago I had been so bewildered and confused that I wanted to talk to Sue, or someone—anyone—perhaps to stop me from what I was about to do. Now I was sure I should go with my new friends in the Lord. I was about to say more to my roommate but my companions kept whispering urgently that we had to leave.

"There's a note inside that explains everything," I said lamely.

Sue hesitated, pondering what she was seeing and what I had just said. Then it seemed as though she decided that nothing unusual was taking place. With a careless wave of her hand, she turned away. "Okay. I'll see you later."

I sat motionless at the wheel until Sue unlocked the door and disappeared inside. "Sister Rachel!" Brother Obadiah said sternly. "We've got to go. We don't dare stay here any longer. Satan still might use your room-mate as a snare to keep you from following God."

"You can't trust the people of the world," Brother Josiah added. "They're in Satan's control and he will use them against you."

"But she's a believer," I protested. "She wants to follow the Lord. She wouldn't be a snare to anyone."

"She *thinks* she's a Christian," he countered.

I glanced at my watch. It was only a few minutes before eleven. I had a sudden desire to see Phil before I left—if nothing else, to tell him goodby. We had meant so much to each other that I felt I had to talk to him one more time, to tell him where I was going and what I would be doing. Maybe he would understand that this new life in Christ was for him, as well as for me.

True, he had always made fun of my faith in Christ and my insistence that I go to Sunday school and church every Sunday. It scarcely seemed likely that he would respond to the persuasiveness of the brothers. Yet, it would be worth a try. Going with Brother Josiah and Brother Obadiah would be a taste of heaven if Phil joined us. I asked about taking the time to see him, but my companions were strongly opposed to it.

"No, Sister!" they protested, almost in one breath. "Going to see this flesh person who has meant so much to you in the past could be a snare to your soul. God is revealing this to you, not to these other people. He isn't calling them. He is calling you. He wants *you* to follow Him now."

"Don't you understand?" Brother Josiah went on. "You are just a babe. You need to study—to become rooted in the Word and to learn more about how to serve

God as He leads you to serve Him. When your faith is strong and solidly established, you can come back and talk to your friends and they will not be able to influence you for evil."

This, I told myself, must be part of the price I had to pay for walking with Christ. After all, the Bible says we should forsake family and friends and possessions to walk with Him. Until now I had only heard people giving assent to that concept. Now, I not only had met two who were actually following Christ's command; I was doing the same thing.

I reached down, turned the ignition key and the motor came to life. As we drove through downtown Kearney, I instinctively glanced at my gas gauge. It registered just below a quarter of a tank. I only had four dollars in my purse, which wouldn't last long the way that Pontiac of mine drank gas.

I didn't know where we were going or how we would get there, unless the brothers had money I didn't know about, but I could wipe concern from my mind. I had a whole new life ahead of me, and God to meet my needs. With a light heart I guided the car along the motel-lined approach to Interstate 80, across the bridge and east on the interchange toward Omaha, Chicago and the East Coast.

And to think! A few hours ago I had been in such a tangled skein of circumstances I felt completely trapped. Now, I was free!

2
My Flesh Family

Driving east along the Interstate I was unnaturally quiet. Although it had been more than a year since I had lived with my parents in Denver, I was conscious of the fact that every mile we traveled took me even farther from them. And, more important, I was embarking on a new life that could mean I would never see them again.

I should have been proud of my dad and mother, but I was not. My resentment against Dad smouldered for taking a printing job at Nebraska Christian High School in Central City when he could have earned twice as much at a secular plant and could have bought me all the things I thought were so necessary as I was growing up.

I was the youngest in our family of five, and was keenly conscious of the fact that money was always scarce. I got most of my clothes from my three older sisters after they had outgrown them. I envied my brother, Tom—at least he didn't have to wear somebody else's castoffs. The rest of the family was able to cope with the situation. But not me.

I remember burning with jealousy when a girl in my class would appear at a party in a new dress or had some new records for her stereo. I used to dream of the day when I would be able to have my own clothes, right from the store, clothes bought especially for me. I wondered what it would be like to see a neat dress or sweater in the window of an exclusive shop in nearby Grand Island, Nebraska, and whip out my very own checkbook to buy it. Some of the kids at Nebraska Christian were from wealthy ranching families, and had their own checking accounts. They could buy almost anything they wanted. To me, they already had the key to a happy, worthwhile life.

I said nothing to anyone else about the way I felt. I smothered my resentment against Dad and offered a smile to the world around me. I didn't once consider the fact that it might be hard for him to see me go without. As far as I was concerned, his stubborn attitude kept me from the happiness I felt was my right.

I realize now that it would have been far better for me to talk out my problems with my parents at the time—to let them know the turmoil that seethed within me. Dad is such a wise, sensitive man that I'm sure he would have been able to help. But I didn't want to hurt him and Mom. For that reason I kept silent, and my bitterness was a cancer in my heart.

I didn't know then that, during their college days, my parents had made a vow to the Lord to never place a price tag on their ministry—they would trust God to provide them with the things they needed. He had been faithful in giving them all the necessities, including those of five growing children. My problem was, I was unwilling to settle for that.

As a young girl, I had received Jesus Christ as my Saviour, but I still had one foot firmly planted in the world. Even while I was establishing a reputation as a model Christian girl the seeds of rebellion were growing.

Had it not been for changing schools, I still might have worked my way out of my spiritual and personal difficulties to a stable Christian maturity. But Dad felt called to become the printer for Western Bible College in Denver. I was uprooted from the relaxed, protected atmosphere of Nebraska Christian High School and dumped into the chaotic worldliness of a public school.

I longed to be popular, to be accepted by the gang of kids who were "somebody" in school. I had always been pretty enough to be popular, especially with the boys. I was petite, almost dainty, with a quick, puckish smile and soft brown eyes the guys found attractive. I soon discovered, however, that it required something more than that. I could not be a part of the gang of kids I longed desperately to be with and still maintain the Christian standards I had been taught. I was soon doing things I knew a believer should not do.

Not that I went against my own convictions—I didn't have any. I had long conformed to what my parents, the church and the Christian high school had taught me without developing any strong principles of my own. The first winds of temptation blew away my feeble defenses and left me vulnerable. It wasn't long until I was scarcely different from the kids I wanted to run with. I maintained a charade of living the Christian life only at home and before the people in the church.

When I graduated from the high school in Colorado my sister, Judy, who was three years older than I, was living in Kearney, preparing to teach school. I decided to move in with her, get a job and save money to go to college. I got a job, but instead of saving anything I began to buy some of those items I had always wanted but couldn't get.

I convinced myself that I had to have a car. After all, I lived quite a distance from work. Then I needed a stereo and some pop albums—I loved music, and a person had to have some enjoyment out of life. Whatever I wanted to do or buy for myself, I was able to find a reason for it.

I even loaned money to some of my friends. I seldom got it back, but I had a hard time refusing them. In spite of my good intentions to save money for college, I spent until I scarcely had enough left to make my payments and take care of my share of the rent and food. Mom and Dad used to get upset about the way I handled my financial affairs and cautioned me to be more careful.

They wanted me to go on to school and knew that I couldn't unless I saved as much as possible. I was well aware that they were speaking the truth but I could do nothing about it—or so it seemed.

I don't know why I was so very different from my sisters and brother in that respect. The oldest, Sharyn, had attended a year at Grace Bible Institute in Omaha before her nurse's training, and had married Jerry Regier, a fellow student. Together, they joined the staff of Campus Crusade for Christ. Marj, just younger than Sharyn, had also earned her way through Bible school and was married to a young minister serving a church in Nampa, Idaho. Tom had gone through college, was married and studying medicine in Omaha. And Judy, next to the youngest, was finishing her education in Kearney, Nebraska at the state college there.

The other kids in the family had been able to learn Dad's and Mom's frugal ways and profit by them. I was the spendthrift, caught up in the love of things and unable to muster the discipline to save for my education.

As long as Judy lived in Kearney and I roomed with her, I was reasonably successful in maintaining the sort of life that would deceive her and my Christian friends and the people in church. She had what I lacked, roots that plunged deep into the Word of God. She lived a separated life, not because people expected it of her as a Martin, but because she had given her heart completely to Jesus Christ. She loved Him and wanted, above all else, to please Him. I went through the motions because I knew they were expected of me, but deep within I knew I was a phony.

Occasionally I chafed under the discipline Judy placed on herself and on me. I had begun to dabble with the world during my last year of high school, doing things I had always been taught were wrong. Despite twinges of guilt, I had found them pleasurable and often wished I didn't have Judy to contend with so I could do as I pleased. I tried not to think too much about the double life I was leading, continuing to go with the gang whenever I had the opportunity and doing whatever they were "into" at the moment.

When Judy graduated and got a teaching job in Davenport, Nebraska, some distance away, my Christian life fell apart. She had been the stabilizing force that kept me from getting too deeply involved in sin. She was my one reason for living the way I had during the year or more I had already been in Kearney. With her gone, my resolve to walk with God was weakened measurably.

I doubt that I ever would have gotten involved with Phil if Judy had stayed in Kearney. I knew from the first time he asked me to go out with him that he wasn't the type of guy a Christian girl should date. He had no use for the church or Jesus Christ. He drank, smoked, and seemed to want a girl for only one reason. Still, I found myself deeply attracted to him.

At first it was exciting to date a sophisticated person like Phil. He was suave and polite and knew how to treat a girl. I felt like a princess when we were together. He was always buying things for me—little pieces of jewelry he knew I would like, expensive perfume, or a box of candy. Our dates were exciting experiences that soon began to end in the back seat of his car.

I became so caught up in my infatuation with him that I could think of nothing else. I was insanely jealous of the other girls in his life and begrudged every minute he spent with them. I used to daydream of introducing myself to them and asking them to give him up so we could be married. I don't know why I thought I had any strong claim on him, or why I even imagined he might marry me, but I did.

Not that the affair with Phil didn't cause me some deep emotional problems. I was a Christian and the terrible reality of what I was doing tore at my soul. God was beginning to close in on Rachel Martin, to bring the fist of His displeasure down on the sin in my life.

That was the way things were when I went home to visit my folks the summer before I met the "brothers." I wanted to talk to my parents, and especially to Dad. Somehow I felt that I had to talk to him, to get him to help me work out the kinks in my spiritual life. Not that I intended to confess to him about Phil. I would have died before I could have told him that. But Dad was gentle and kind and wise. Somehow I felt that he would have the answer to my problems.

When I rode out to Denver by train, however, Sharyn and Jerry were there with their children and Dad had a rush print job he had to get finished on Saturday. I went over to the shop to talk with him while he worked. I longed to tell him how deeply troubled I was, but how could I do that with the printing press clanging and him working frantically so he could get the job done? He wanted to go home and be with the rest of the family.

I don't know what might have happened if we could have talked seriously. Perhaps I would have gotten my life straightened out and would not have listened to the brothers. As it was, I wore my best mask of gaiety. No one could possibly have known that my heart was bleeding.

When we got back to the house there was the usual excitement of a home bustling with family. We talked and laughed a lot, but never very seriously.

That night, long after everyone else was asleep, I lay in bed, my troubled conscience tearing at me. A certain desperation seized me. I knew that, whatever happened, I had to see Dad alone before I went back to Kearney sometime the next afternoon.

But the conversation I longed for was not to take place. We went to church in the morning, after getting up a bit later than usual. There was so much confusion that I had no opportunity to talk with Dad. And that afternoon, shortly after dinner, Sharyn's little boy fell, hitting his head on the side of the car. Dad and Jerry took him to the hospital for emergency treatment and just as they got back, my ride came for me. I kept my friends waiting long enough to rush into the house and the folks' bedroom where I pinned a note on the pillow. I didn't realize it then, but I had written a desperate plea for help.

"I was really disappointed that I didn't get to talk to you . . ." I wrote.

I was hurt and bewildered. Now I was on my way back to Kearney without having had a chance to talk to Dad about the heaviness of my heart. I was beginning to feel trapped—boxed in until there was no way of escape for me.

About a month later, I wrote the folks a card from Washington, D.C. when Sue and I were visiting Sharyn and Jerry there. That was the last they were to hear from me, except for three widely-spaced letters I wrote while traveling with the group, and the phone call from Tom informing them of my disappearance.

Mom told me later that Dad's face went ashen as my brother explained what had happened. "It's Rae." (He always called me by my family nickname.) "She's disappeared."

"What do you mean?" The fear in Dad's heart was mirrored in his eyes and Mom read it with concern.

"Sue phoned me. She said that Rae took some of her things and left the apartment with two strange men. There was a note that said something about going off to serve God."

I'm sure there was more to the conversation, but that's all Dad remembers. He was trembling with emotion as he hung up the phone and groped for a chair.

3
"God Will Provide"

I was still driving east with my robed companions when the sputtering of the car engine rudely jerked my attention from the spiritual plane of our conversation to more worldly concerns, like money and running out of gas. We had already spent my four dollars for fuel and were beginning to run low again. If we didn't get more in a few minutes we would be stalled along the highway.

"What are we going to do now?" I asked, lacking the faith of Brothers Josiah and Obadiah that everything would work out.

"Take the next exit and pull in to the service station," the dark-haired Brother Obadiah instructed me.

I lifted my foot from the accelerator and followed the orange reflectors that marked the exit. I was able to make out the darkened service station on the opposite side of the north-south road, but I could not see how stopping there would help our situation. "It's closed," I protested, surprised that they had not noticed that important fact. And besides, I had already spent everything I had. "Unless you've got some money, we're not going to be able to buy any gas, even if we find a place that's open."

That didn't seem to bother my companions. They told me to park where they could reach the tank with both hoses.

"Why?" I asked, apprehensively. I wondered if they

were planning to break into the station. My heart raced.

"There's always a little gas left in each hose," Brother Josiah explained, patiently. As he did so he inserted the nozzle into the gullet of the hungry car. "We only get a little from each pump, but a station as large as this will have a gallon or two for us. Like we were saying a few minutes ago, 'God will provide.' "

Once we finished draining the hoses we went back to the highway and drove to the next exit. No one mentioned it, but it was apparent to me that we would have to stop again and again, if that was to be the way we got our gas. We hadn't found enough at that station to take us more than a few miles.

We had stopped on the platform of another closed station when a buzzer sounded raucously and dogs began to bark. I panicked—although the brothers had assured me that what we were doing was not illegal and was God's way of providing for us, I was sure the place would soon be swarming with police. I was terrified, and prayed that God would help us to get away before we were caught. We careened out of the driveway and back onto the broad highway just as the manager, who must have lived in the back or in a house we hadn't noticed next door, switched on the lights.

"Praise the Lord," Brother Josiah murmured.

Although they professed to believe we were doing nothing wrong and were not concerned, I noticed that the brothers kept looking back to see if we were being followed. We were just beginning to relax when five police cars came speeding up, their lights flashing.

My heart hammered violently as I pulled over to the side of the road and stopped. My folks had taught me to respect the law, and until that moment I had never even received a traffic ticket. Now I could see myself in jail. That wasn't the way things were supposed to turn out, I reasoned. I had gone with Brother Obadiah and Brother Josiah in my desire to serve God completely. It wasn't to end this way, in humiliation and defeat.

"Don't be upset, Sister," Brother Obadiah whispered from the back seat. "The Lord will take care of this. He always has."

As the officer approached, both of my companions got out of the car. After the preliminary request for identification and the statement that we had the right to remain silent, one of the troopers questioned us about stealing gas.

"We weren't stealing," Brother Obadiah protested. "As followers of Jesus Christ, we keep the law."

That seemed to disturb the officer in charge. "Now, wait a minute," he broke in. "You stopped at that station up the road, didn't you?"

Brother Obadiah admitted that we had.

"And you saw that it was closed before you pulled in and stopped. If you weren't going to break in, why did you do that?"

"We expected God to provide for us."

The officer had not expected such an answer. "What do you guys do?" he demanded.

"We're Christians," my new friends explained patiently, in much the same tone they had used to answer my questions. "We're preachers of the Word. We just travel around, telling people about Jesus."

I was astonished at how calm and undisturbed they were in the face of this terrible development. I didn't see how they could be so relaxed. They acted as though they were sure God was going to see them through this trial, and if He didn't, that He would give them the grace and strength and courage to take going to jail. I prayed for the faith they had, but it was no use. I was still as frightened as ever.

"A minute ago you said you had stopped at the station because you expected God to provide for you. Just what did you think He would do to give you gas?"

For the first time there was an instant's hesitation. Then Brother Josiah related what we had done at the first station. That was what we had planned on doing when we stopped a second time.

"And you don't call that stealing?" The officer was incredulous.

"Of course not," Brother Obadiah who was the spokesman on this occasion, retorted quickly. "We just took the gas that was in the hose—gas that was extra and was being wasted."

"Somebody paid for that gas," the trooper reminded him, "and tomorrow morning the first customer to stop at the pumps where you drained the hoses will have to fill them again, but he won't be able to get that gas. He's the person you were stealing from."

My companions seemed surprised, as though the thought had never occurred to them.

"What are you going to do in the morning when you run out again?" another officer broke in. "Will you stop somewhere else and help yourself the way you have tonight?"

"I don't know," Brother Josiah replied, truthfully. "We will probably find something to sell."

The officers got on the radio after questioning us and had the dispatcher phone the manager of the first station to see if he wanted to press charges. While they were waiting for an answer, two troopers had me get out and go with them to one of the state cars where I was beyond the hearing of my two companions.

"How old are you, Miss?" they asked me.

"Twenty." I was so frightened my voice trembled, and I spoke so softly they had to ask me to repeat.

They looked me over. I was dressed in jeans and a sweat shirt, which must have seemed weird in view of the robes and sandals of my companions.

"Do you really want to be with these men?"

"I think so," I answered without conviction. After all that had happened that night, I wasn't sure of anything.

I expected them to stop questioning me when I told them I was going voluntarily. The very fact that I was driving when they stopped us proved as much. Still, they were not satisfied. They wanted to know if my folks were aware of where I was and what I was doing.

"No," I said, honestly, "but they know that God is taking care of me and they want me in His will."

"At twenty, she should know what she's doing," one of the officers muttered, his voice edged with frustration. "Besides, she's of age. If she wants to be with those creeps, there's nothing we can do about it."

By this time the dispatcher got back to the officers. He had reached the station manager and the man didn't want to press charges. We had gotton less than a dollar's worth of gas from the pumps at his station and he didn't feel he could have us jailed for that. The brothers were told that we could go. "Only don't drain any more gas out of the hoses at gas stations," the officer in charge warned.

Brother Obadiah and Brother Josiah both promised that we wouldn't and got into the car again as the state police drove away.

"You see, Sister," Josiah said when we were moving once more, "God takes care of us." He did not mention that we had been spared arrest only because the station manager felt our theft had been too small to cause us trouble. "We really shouldn't blame the officers or the station manager who reported us. They are of the world and simply don't understand our way of life or how God looks after us."

We had only traveled a mile or two when we saw the lights of an all-night service station just ahead. Brother Obadiah asked if I had a spare tire. "If you do, we'd better sell it to get some gas."

The decision proved wise. We were just pulling off at the exit when the car sputtered and jerked to a halt. "I'll take the tire down to the station," Brother Josiah said cheerfully, "and see what kind of deal I can make."

"Praise the Lord," Brother Obadiah replied. That seemed to be a stock answer for any situation.

A few minutes later a service truck came out, pushed

us into the station and put five dollars' worth of gas in the car in exchange for the tire and wheel. We wouldn't be able to go far, I reasoned, but at least we weren't stranded. Perhaps this was the way the Lord worked, taking us one step without showing us how He was going to get us to our ultimate destination. I began to feel the excitement of what was happening. It was a thrill just to anticipate how God would work the next time.

By now we were getting close to Lincoln. Even though we were on the Interstate, we were driving through rolling hills that marked our approach to the capital city. We were all tired and the brothers began to talk about stopping somewhere to sleep.

This moment had been nudging into the back of my mind since we left the state troopers. I wondered which one would suggest sleeping with me and how he would try to justify it. That was the sort of thing I could have expected from most of the guys I knew. At least Brothers Josiah and Obahiah would not be suggesting that we go to a motel. They didn't have any money for that. But I waited with growing apprehension.

"Sister," one of the brothers instructed when we reached a quiet exit not far from Lincoln, "pull off here and we'll sleep for awhile."

My knuckles showed white on the steering wheel and my back was straight and tense. I should have known better than to leave Kearney with two men I had never seen before. What else could I expect? And how would I be able to fight them off? They had chosen a lonely area where no one would hear my screams. My heart cried out to God as I drove off the road, mechanically, and stopped.

As soon as I shut off the engine the back doors opened and both brothers got out. "Sister Rachel," Brother Obadiah said quietly, "you can sleep in the car. We'll be close by if you need us." They took their packs and went to a grassy spot twenty or thirty feet away.

I stared incredulously at them. I had not expected to be treated with such consideration. They called themselves my brothers and I was their sister, both in their thinking and in the way they treated me. As we talked about stopping for the night I had been sure they had other things in mind.

However, they accorded me the same respect my flesh brother, Tom, would have. I curled up in the back seat and closed my eyes, thanking God for what had happened and for the strong moral character and consideration of my companions. Their attitude toward me that first night did much to convince me of their spiritual depth and sincerity.

4
On The Road

The next morning we drove on to Omaha. It was traumatic for me to be in the city where my only brother, Tom, lived. Doubts began to creep in and I longed to see him and get his counsel. He was older than I and a dedicated believer. I had always trusted his judgment.

My companions saw that I was disturbed and wanted to know why. I shared with them my wish to see my brother, if only for a few minutes. Brothers Obadiah and Josiah had been so kindly I was sure they would understand and grant my request.

"Every one of us had to go through this sort of thing," they reasoned patiently. "It is difficult to leave our flesh people and everything we have known all our lives, but it is for the Lord." They gave me time to think about that—to accept their wisdom. "Just remember, Sister, you're not doing this for us, or for yourself. It is all for the Lord."

I tried to accept the things they were saying, but there was little comfort for me in their rationalizing. They knew more about the Bible and living dedicated lives than I could ever know, but even that was of no help. Tears filled my eyes as I realized that I probably would never see any of the members of my family again. The tears clung to my lashes momentarily, then scorched their way down my cheeks. I tried desperately to turn my thoughts from Tom and his lovely wife, but I could not.

In spite of my own rebellion we had always been a close family. I had not fully understood how close we were until now—now, when I was turning my back on them.

"Couldn't I please talk to Tom?" I pleaded, desperately. "If I could just see him for a minute or two so I could tell him where I'm going and who I'm with, it would help so much. My parents wouldn't worry about me."

But Brother Josiah was firm. "You have forsaken all and are following Jesus. You know what the Bible says about the person who puts his hand to the plow and then turns back. Like we said, most people feel this way in the beginning. It is a pulling of your flesh people—a snare of Satan."

"Your flesh brother could be the snare to keep you from following the leading of God," Brother Obadiah went on. "This is a decision we all have to make. Your flesh people are the worst snares of all because you are so close to them and have loved them so much. They have such a hold on you that they can easily drag your flesh back into the conveniences of the world. They don't really love *you*, Sister Rachel. They only love your flesh. If you are going to live for God you will have to put them out of your life."

I could not believe what they were trying to tell me about my family. It sounded as though they were trying to depict my parents and sisters and brother as my worst enemies. And that could not be. They loved me. And not just my flesh. They truly loved me and were concerned about me.

I was not able to argue with Brothers Josiah and Obadiah, especially when they sprinkled their conversation with quotations from the Bible, but I knew my family's love to be true. Silently, I wondered what my robed companions would say if they knew I had tucked several pictures of my family in the bottom of my purse before leaving my apartment in Kearney.

"You have to think of your soul, Sister," they

persisted. "That is the only thing that counts. If you are not doing what God wants you to, your soul is doomed for Hell."

I challenged them on that statement. I had received Christ when I was seven and had been taught in the Scriptures that I was saved by grace for all eternity. "Our works don't save us," I concluded.

"What you say is true, but if you don't continue to walk in the way the Lord teaches you, you're not going to make it into the Kingdom. It might not be pleasant to think about, but it's in the Word of God."

I was so confused and bewildered by everything that was happening and the way in which they used the Bible to prove the things they were saying that I didn't know what I believed. I would question them often in my own mind, but at the same time I was so overwhelmed by their apparent knowledge of the Bible and the assurance with which they spoke, that I remained silent. I had to have time to think.

Since we had no more money and nothing else left to sell to get money for gas, the brothers decided to dispose of my car. But that was not easily done. Although I had paid $700 for it six months earlier and had not put all that many miles on it, the best offer they could get for it was $125. I think the used car dealers must have taken one look at their robes and decided that my friends would sell the car for any ridiculous figure they were offered.

"There's no use in our trying any more," Brother Josiah said wearily, after spending half a day driving from one car lot to another. "No one is going to give us what the car is worth. We're going to have to park it somewhere for awhile."

"Like where?" Brother Obadiah wanted to know.

"The parking lot at the Medical Center. You know, we went by there this morning."

Brother Josiah turned at the next corner and we parked the car in the center of the lot. My heart leaped as we locked it and walked away. This was the place where

Tom went to school. He and Janell must live nearby. I glanced around, wildly, as we crossed the street. Perhaps if I broke away from the brothers and ran toward the houses, jammed one against the other, I could find Tom's place and get to talk to him.

But, even as the impulse seized me I realized that I could not do as I felt compelled to. The brothers had forbidden me even to talk to my flesh brother. I could not disobey them. All I had been able to accomplish in the last few miserable years of my life was to get into a terrible, tangled mess. Now I was leaving all the sin behind and was going to serve Christ. I could not turn back.

During a brief rest, torn by bewilderment and doubt, I picked up my Bible and began to read how some of the disciples who followed Jesus went back to their homes, sold everything they had, and brought the proceeds to Jesus' feet. I leaped at that. It was a way of turning back, if only for a few hours . . . a way I could return to Kearney and talk to my roommate . . . a way I could tell those I loved where I was going and why.

"Brothers," I exclaimed, reading the verses aloud, "I have to go back and sell everything so I can turn the money over to Jesus. That is exactly what the disciples did."

I waited, hopefully, for their approval, but it didn't come. "Sister," Brother Obadiah said patiently, "every situation is different. You were deep in sin when you lived in Kearney. You had to get out of there. You had so many friends who could pull you back into your old life. To go back now would be to turn your back on Jesus Christ."

He opened the Bible to another passage of Scripture and read the account of one who sought to follow Jesus. He wanted to become a disciple, but asked Jesus Christ if he could go back, first, and wait until after his father died. Then he would leave what he had and walk with Jesus. " 'Let the dead bury their dead,' Christ answered. That verse applies to you, Sister. You have to press on with us."

Reluctantly I closed my Bible and resigned myself to leaving Omaha without seeing my flesh brother. As we got up to move on, I seemed to be caught up by a force outside myself, propelled along a course I wasn't sure I wanted to walk. Step by step I was getting farther away from Tom and Janell and the rest of my flesh people. An awful feeling of emptiness swept over me. I could not have felt worse if I had suddenly been confronted with the news that they had all been involved in a terrible accident and had been killed. The situation was much the same. By my own actions I was separating myself from them.

Yet, in spite of the desolation and the aching in my heart, I was committed to a course I had to follow. I was firmly convinced that God had led me to go with the brothers. I could not turn back.

Still, I was disturbed by the agony I was experiencing. I had always accepted the fact that walking with Christ was a happy, joyous way of life. If that were true, why did I feel so terrible? I suddenly became concerned about keeping my hurt from my companions. Furtively I brushed at my eyes, trying to wipe away the tears that welled there, before anyone saw them.

I had no idea where we were going or when we would get there. I had asked the brothers about our destination once before, when we were back in Kearney, but they had given me a vague answer that told me nothing.

I was thinking about our unannounced destination when we were picked up by a van on the edge of Omaha and were given a ride some distance into Iowa. The vehicle was owned by some Jesus organization that was working in the Nebraska metropolis. As soon as we got into the vehicle the guys who were driving it tried to share Christ with us.

I listened intently as they discussed the Word of God, but my companions were guarded and suspicious. They even refused to look at the tracts our benefactors tried to give them. "We don't need those," Brother Josiah informed them proudly. "You can take them back. The Lord has revealed to us that we need to get out of this world in order to be what He wants us to be."

"That's right," Brother Obadiah added. "We want to serve God with all our hearts."

After we were let out, Brother Josiah turned to me with a warning. "There are a lot of people like that around the country. They think they are Christians, but they ride around in immodest clothing and possess things like that van. They are being foolish, selfish, covetous and greedy over *things*."

We spent the night in a field along the Interstate in western Iowa. It was a beautiful evening with the moon riding high over the peaceful prairies and the stars gleaming down at us. The brothers knew I was lonely and did what they could to cheer me. We sat in the stillness for a long while, talking quietly, if at all.

"I was heavy into Satanism before I met Brother Evangelist and the group," Brother Josiah said. "I was freed from the power of sin. It's wonderful to know the Lord and to be delivered from a terrible lie like Satanism."

I could understand something of how he felt. I knew how I had been weighted down by the burden of sin. The pressure gets so heavy a person would do most anything to be rid of it.

Then the other told his story. Brother Obadiah had been a singer with a rock group before turning his life completely over to God. He knew what it was to have girls throw themselves at him. He knew the wild fantasies of drugs and the compelling hold liquor could place upon a person. He, too, had also known peace for the first time in his life after receiving Christ and forsaking the world.

Their stories thrilled me and made me even more sure than ever that I had chosen the right course. We talked some more and one of the brothers took a robe from his own pack and asked me to put it on.

"A woman should cover herself modestly," he said. "It is ungodly for you to wear pants like a man."

I wasn't sure that I agreed entirely with what he was saying, and especially that the sort of jeans I had on were men's clothing. As far as I could tell they were made definitely for women. But I wanted to go all the way with God. There were to be no more reservations in my life, I decided—no hanging back. If that meant wearing a robe rather than jeans, I was going to wear a robe, no matter how I felt about it personally.

I pulled on the robe over my other clothes, grimacing at the shapeless shadow I made in the dying sunlight. *It is modest, all right,* I concluded to myself. *As modest as wearing a tent.* But I kept thinking that I was doing it for God. That made it all right.

Time was a blur to me. The hours became days and the days a week as we continued to hitchhike across the central United States. My companions were heading for a specific point or were traveling a predetermined route. That was apparent from the decisive way in which they changed highways at certain cities or towns. There was no discussion about where to go next—no indecision. We had to be following a certain, prescribed course.

When I first left Kearney with the brothers I was quite concerned about having enough food to eat, since they had told me they had no money. When I revealed my fears, they chided me gently. "Don't you trust God?" they asked. "Don't you believe Him when He says that we're not to take thought for tomorrow—that we're not to worry about what we should eat or wear?"

"Yes," I acknowledged, "I believe Him, but—"

"We either trust Christ or we don't," Brother Josiah reminded me, pointedly. "Don't worry. We'll have plenty to eat."

I wanted to ask how he could be so sure, but that would only further expose my lack of trust. So I waited in silence, wondering. It wasn't long until I understood what he meant, although at first I found it difficult to eat what they brought to me.

They went behind the busier restaurants and supermarkets in the cities we passed through and raided the garbage pails. I was astonished by the amount and variety of food that was thrown away. Only the fact that we were eating garbage tore at me. My stomach churned. Brother Josiah and Brother Obadiah both saw that my face wrinkled distastefully, and it must have taken on a greenish tinge.

"Sister," Brother Josiah said, his voice as stern and harsh as the set of his jaw, "the Bible tells us that we are to eat what has been set before us without question or hesitation. God has provided for us. This is what He has given us to eat. Do we dare indicate our displeasure? Are we to be like the Israelites, complaining about the manna God provided for them when he was leading them through the wilderness? Is that to be the way you show Him your appreciation?"

I cringed under the cold, expressionless glare in his eyes. I swallowed hard, and with an unspoken prayer for strength and an iron stomach, I took a bite. I thought I would never be able to swallow it, but somehow I managed to get it down. And, more important, it stayed down. The next bite was no better, but finally I had eaten enough to sate my hunger. After a time I was able to eat what they scrounged without difficulty.

There was nothing wrong with the food. The difficulty was in my mind, caused by an overactive imagination and what I had been taught as I grew up. Garbage, around our house, was for pigs or the dog and cat. We were frugal in what we prepared, in order to make the food budget stretch as far as possible, but once something was consigned to the garbage pail it stayed there.

The brothers didn't take food that had been partially eaten, the scrapings off plates, or that which had spoiled.

Everything they took was clean and edible and often quite tasty.

Behind the stores we found fruit that was too ripe to carry over for another day, and bread and cottage cheese and ice cream that had gone beyond the resale date. Behind the cafes, and especially the quick food places such as McDonald's and Burger King, we found hamburgers that had been fried but were unsold, and rolls that were still good but were getting dry and hard.

In all the time I was with the group I can't remember ever being really hungry when we went to bed. At times our diet was bland and monotonous. It wasn't very exciting when we had stale bread or aging cottage cheese to eat for three days in a row, but when that happened we thought of the Children of Israel and thanked God that we could experience the same monotony they experienced as they traveled through the wilderness, existing on manna, month after month. We counted it a privilege to have to suffer, even in such a small way, for Christ. We told ourselves that it was good for us to have to sacrifice. I honestly don't believe that it hurt any of us to eat the way we did, except that our diet was heavy on starches and we had a definite lack of vitamins.

Running out of gas, trying to sell the car, having to stop frequently to look for food, and finding rides for three, made traveling slow. But after a week or more, a new excitement seemed to grip the brothers. I didn't quite understand and didn't feel that I should ask why, but their pace seemed to quicken and their spirits lifted. Then one morning Brother Obadiah told me the reason for their excitement. He came over to the place where I was sleeping and wakened me with the news that we were not far from the rest of the group.

"Sister Rachel," he said, his voice taut with emotion, "we've been seeing signs for the last day or two that some of our group have been this way. Now we've found a place where the grass has been crushed down. Some brothers must have slept here, and not too long ago."

All that morning they talked about the group and how wonderful it would be to be rejoined with them. They made it sound as though being with the others would be closely akin to being in Heaven.

"I wish I could find the words to tell you how wonderful it will be," Brother Obadiah said. "You will soon be meeting the blessed sisters. You can't imagine what they are like or the love they have for each other. The peace and joy and happiness they know is like nothing you have ever experienced before."

"You talked about the love in your flesh family," Brother Josiah added pointedly. "Wait until you experience being with the other sisters. The harmony they enjoy can be found nowhere else on this earth."

The way they talked made me so eager to be with the group I didn't even want to take time to eat. I began to realize that this was what I had been waiting for. I had never been so happy about joining Brothers Obadiah and Josiah as I was at that moment.

By this time we were nearing Iowa City, Iowa. Instead of stopping at dark as we usually had done, we kept hitchhiking. We caught a ride late at night and finally, in the early predawn hours, we were let out at an exit near the city.

"It is late," Brother Josiah said. "Perhaps it would be better for us to rest for awhile and meet the others in the morning."

Brother Obadiah took some food from his pack and shared it with Brother Josiah and me. Then we unrolled our bedrolls and lay down, the brothers some distance away. I don't know about my companions, but for me, sleep was unthinkable. I was too excited about the prospect of meeting the others in the group.

5
The Group

As I lay in my sleeping bag watching the eastern skies lighten, turn silver and finally gold, my fears and doubts rushed back.

In a few short hours we would be with the others. What would that be like? Would they accept me as one of them, or would I have to remain on the fringe? All my life I had been plagued with feelings of inferiority. I had been frank and honest in sharing my own unworthiness with the brothers and it hadn't seemed to matter to them. But what about the others? How would they treat me when they learned the truth about me?

At that moment my concern was not whether I was doing what was right or wrong. I was upset by the unknown. I was aware that I was walking an unfamiliar path. Since leaving Kearney, I had grown accustomed to Brother Obadiah and Brother Josiah. I knew they accepted me. But would the rest of the men show me the same respect? And what about the girls? Would they look down on me, or would I be one of them?

I thought my questions were innocent enough. I wanted to know how many were in the group, how many single girls I would be with, how many married couples, and if there were any children. As I lay there thinking, I realized that I knew absolutely nothing about anyone in the group—not even Brothers Obadiah and Josiah.

They had not once used their "flesh names" as they

called them, nor had they said where they were from. I didn't know how old they were, if they had graduated from high school or if they had graduate degrees. Their grammar, use of words, and diction indicated that they were intelligent and well educated, but that was all I could surmise about them. I didn't even know for sure what they looked like, except that they were tall and had a gaunt, emaciated look. Their faces were hidden behind their full beards and their frames were shrouded in dirty gray robes. Once or twice I indicated that I would like to know their real names, but they refused to tell me even that much about themselves.

"Our old lives are behind us," they informed me, "so we have been given new names, like they did in Bible times."

They did talk about Brother Evangelist, Jim Roberts, and brothers John and James and Timothy, and sisters Lydia and Priscilla and Faith and Hope. They mentioned, on one occasion, that there were some married couples in the group and I guessed that there was a child or two. But that was all.

Confused and frustrated, I called out to the Lord as I lay, sleepless and fearful, "God, I want to do what is right. Help me to know."

As I prayed, it seemed that a quietness took hold of me. My fears calmed and I felt that I was in the center of God's will. I was sure, then, that I would truly find Christian love and fellowship and spiritual strength in the group.

About noon we arrived at the public camping area where the group was gathered. My first indication that we had finally reached the place where the others were camped came as we left the road and made our way down the grassy, tree-shaded slope toward a picnic table. Through the autumn leaves I caught a glimpse of the robed figure of a man sitting on one of the benches. My heart leaped and I almost grasped Brother Josiah by the arm.

"Is that one of the other brothers?" I whispered.

He nodded wordlessly.

I was quite unprepared for what happened next. I was so excited at finally meeting up with the rest of the group that I could scarcely control myself. Had I followed my first impulse I might have rushed over to the robed stranger and thrown my arms around him in greeting, I was so happy. But I had been with Brothers Obadiah and Josiah long enough to know that such conduct was not considered proper.

Still, I expected some warmth in the way my companions were welcomed by him. They had told me so much about the love the members of the group had for each other and had stressed how much deeper that love was than the love between members of our flesh families. The brother sitting at the table looked up as we approached and I thought he would jump to his feet and embrace the brothers, but he did not move. He grunted something unintelligible, but his expression did not change—nor was there recognition or joy in his eyes.

"Praise God, Brother," my companions said in a lifeless monotone, quite unlike the way they talked when the three of us had been alone. "Where's camp?"

He looked up from his Bible long enough to point toward a wooded area on the opposite side of the shallow ravine. "Over there," he murmured.

I glanced quickly at my companions to see their reaction to his unfriendliness, but they acted as though it were normal. They picked up their packs and started on. I lingered behind, disturbed by the lack of friendliness and joy. It didn't seem right, somehow, for us to come into camp where the others were and to be greeted this way.

The brother we had just met looked as forlorn and helpless to me as a poor, lost kitten in a late fall rain. His robe-shrouded torso sagged and his eyes were dull and expressionless. He looked to be under twenty-two or three, but, huddled on the picnic bench, he could have

ESCAPE

been twice that. It might have been the beard but I could read only despair in his pallid, whiskered face. I didn't think I had ever seen anyone so miserable.

A line from a hymn we used to sing at church back home came to mind. "...There is joy in serving Jesus..." That was the way I remembered the song. But there didn't seem to be much joy in that brother's life. I couldn't help wondering if he had just learned about something terrible that had happened at home, or if he had been severely chastised for some sin in his life, or if he was just lonely and homesick. It couldn't have anything to do with his flesh family, I decided. The members of the group had put their parents and brothers and sisters out of their lives and hearts.

Perhaps it was just his way and nothing out of the ordinary at all, I thought. But I had to do something to show him I cared. I had nothing to give him, and his attitude indicated that he did not want to talk to me. I was about to go on when I remembered the apple I still had. Brother Josiah had picked some from an orchard we passed and I still had one that I had been saving for supper that night. Impulsively, I took it over to the one on the bench.

"Brother," I said, softly, "do you want an apple?"

His unhappy eyes met mine. "Thank you."

I held it out for him to take but he pulled his hand away quickly, before our fingers touched. Then, with certain caution, he extended his hand so he could take the apple with the tips of his fingers without running the risk of touching me. I didn't understand what that was all about, but I knew it had something to do with the stiff moral code the group had set for themselves. We were not supposed to touch each other, even casually.

I hurried to catch up with Brother Obadiah and Brother Josiah, still trying to sort out the strange actions of the young man we had just met. His ways were really weird, I decided, but perhaps I would learn one day the reasons behind his strange manners. I certainly couldn't figure them out right then.

When we got to the main camp the brothers crowded around my companions. Here I began to see a measure of the love I had expected. We were walking along the narrow path when we began to meet the brothers, one or two at a time. They threw their arms about each other and embraced with a "holy kiss" as the Bible calls it. Although it was foreign to me and I must admit a bit embarrassing, I felt the fellowship and closeness, one with another, that I had expected to see when we met the others. It all seemed so tender—so holy.

I was not introduced to any of them, but that was of small matter. I had already learned that the women in the group were to be subservient to the men. A few weeks before I would have rebelled, bitterly, but now I accepted the situation as it was. If that was what the Bible taught—and both Brother Josiah and Brother Obadiah said that it was—then I wanted to follow that precept.

As we made our way up the slope I saw that most of the men were bearded. With their long robes and unshaven faces I could think only of the men in the Bible. Without closing my eyes I could imagine that we were back in Jerusalem at the time of Christ. Peter and Paul and John would be there, along with our Lord Jesus. The bond between the disciples must have been very similar to the bond I was seeing between the brothers. It made me glad that I had left Kearney and joined the group.

We went on a few yards to the gentle slope where the unmarried sisters had pitched their tents. As we approached, I realized that there must have been twice as many men as girls in the group. Some of the sisters were sitting cross-legged, sewing, while others were in the same position, reading their Bibles. The hush over the camp was amazing to me. I heard no voices, no laughter, and I saw few smiles.

I don't know why, but my first thought was of the pictures I had seen of Indian encampments. The women would be sitting in front of their teepees, taking care of the children, or sewing or scraping hides. There were no children playing around these tents, but the rest of the scene was strikingly similar.

At first the sisters remained where they were, eyeing me shyly, but making no move to come over and speak to me. Then, as though having received some sort of silent communication from one of the brothers, a girl about my own age laid aside the robe she was sewing on and came over to meet me. She put her arms around me and kissed me.

"Praise God!" she exclaimed. "Welcome, Sister."

Another followed suit, and another and another. It did not stop until I had been welcomed by all of them. For me it was a glorious experience. The doubts that had overwhelmed me from time to time were engulfed in the warmth of the greeting I had just received. My heart went out to the sisters, just as their hearts went out to me. Tears of gratitude and joy trickled down my cheeks.

"We will leave you here now," Brother Obadiah said. "The sisters will show you where you will sleep and help you get situated."

I put my bedroll in the tent I was directed to and watched, motionless, as my companions for the trip from Kearney went back to the brothers' camp. When they were out of sight I turned slowly to survey the place where I would be living until it was decided that we should move on.

Until that moment I hadn't noticed the squalor of the camp, or the smell of body odors. I saw, too, that the sisters were not as clean as I had expected them to be. Their hands were begrimed and their nails darkened with dirt. Their faces were sweaty, their tunics stained and threadbare. In spite of myself and the warmth of the greeting I had just received, I recoiled slightly. I didn't care where we traveled or what happened, I thought, but I could never allow myself to get like that.

The instant I harbored such a thought I was shamed

by it. *How could I be so critical?* I asked myself. I didn't know what it was like living in a tent and trying to cook and sew on the bare ground. Besides, Jesus told us that we were to look at the inward person. I was to concern myself with the souls of the sisters, not with their outward appearance.

The other girls must have felt the same revulsion at the lack of cleanliness when they first arrived. The fact that they were able to conquer those feelings was an indication that God did not want us to concern ourselves about such things. I would have to pray much that He would give me the grace to accept the situation the way it was without criticizing or finding fault. This, I determined, must be God's will for my life. He would give me the strength I needed to be as content and happy as the others were.

One of the sisters took me on a brief tour of the camp. "We really don't have all that much to do," she explained. "We take care of all the cooking for ourselves and the brothers and help look after the children when there are any with us. And we do the sewing and patching and mending. The rest of the time we have free to read the Bible and pray."

That sounded idyllic to me. I had never spent the time in the Word that I should have, although that was no fault of my parents. It would be tremendous to have hours and hours every day to spend in His Word.

A hot breeze stirred the air and I became aware of the weight of the robe over my jeans and top. I suddenly realized that I hadn't had a bath or changed clothes since we left Kearney. I was uncomfortably warm and tired from traveling. A bath sounded wonderful.

"Where do you take your baths?" I asked.

"Down at the lake."

My face must have registered my surprise.

"We bathe with our clothes on," the sister added quickly.

"How can you get clean?" I asked, my nose wrinkling

distastefully.

She had no answer for me.

"Sometimes," another sister said, "we go into town to the university and use the showers. That's really neat. Only . . ."

"Only what?"

"Only you have to be careful if you do that. You have to act as though you go to school there and sort of sneak in."

I turned that over in my mind. It didn't sound quite right to me for a Christian to be so deceitful. "Is that honest?"

"It doesn't hurt anybody," she replied. "The showers are there and the hot water is there. The brothers say that is part of God's provision for us."

The shower sounded much better to me than trying to bathe in the lake with my clothes on, but I didn't know whether I was ready to try sneaking into one of the girls' dorms at Iowa U to shower, in spite of what I had been told.

Word of my desire to take a bath must have become known. It wasn't long until a girl who was called Sister Dorcas identified herself. "I'm going to the lake to wash some clothes," she told me. "You can go along, if you like, and take your bath there."

"Thank you, Sister," I said, gratefully.

Suddenly I realized that I was wearing the only clothes I had and that I would have to return the robe to Brother Josiah. That left me with my sinful jeans and top.

Sister Dorcas must have read the consternation in my eyes. "I have an extra skirt for you, Sister Rachel."

Another gave me a blouse to wear. Now I would be properly outfitted after my bath in the lake. At first I thought they were only being kind. Later, I was to learn that they were merely expressing the communal philosophy of the group owning everything and individuals being permitted to use what they needed.

I discovered that Sister Dorcas was not going to be washing alone. Sister Miriam went along to help. They picked up their buckets and dirty clothes and went down to the pump by the lake a short distance from camp. I trudged behind. I wanted to help carry something but they wouldn't let me. "You're still tired from traveling," Sister Dorcas said. "You can help when you're rested."

I didn't protest. I hadn't realized, until we reached our destination, exactly how tired I was. Muscles and joints I didn't know I had ached fiercely.

"I should have brought the case for my contacts down here with me," I said as we neared the water. "I don't want to risk losing them."

"I used to wear contacts," Sister Miriam said, "but when I came to serve the Lord with the group He showed me that He would heal my eyes if He wanted me to see. He spoke to me about the foolishness of trusting in man's inventions."

I couldn't understand what she was trying to say. "Everybody wears glasses."

"That doesn't make it right. When God dealt with me I forsook my contacts. He helps me to see what I need to see."

There was more I wanted to ask her but by this time we had reached the pump and Sister Dorcas had started to wash clothes by hand. The two of them were soon on their knees struggling with those heavy robes, trying to get them clean, and I was amazed that they actually seemed happy doing their washing that way. If they weren't happy, at least they didn't seem to mind the inconveniences.

I thought I could understand the reason. If we were to be free from all those wicked inventions—those entrapments of Satan—we had to be inconvenienced, at least to some extent. Everything we did for God cost something. The freedom and time to study the Bible were worth the difficulties in washing clothes.

When the task was almost finished, Sister Miriam

went on down to the lake with me. Still wearing the robe, I waded into the water and managed to take off the jeans and top and bathe with the robe on. As the cool water eased away the grime of days of travel and sleeping in the open, I thought about the conversation I had had with Sister Miriam about her contact lenses.

All my life I had been taught that we, as believers, should trust the Lord. I had heard my parents and our pastor talk about God's miraculous healing power. That was what I wanted for myself. It would be wonderful to have my full sight restored.

Inevitably, my attention was drawn to Sister Miriam. I noticed how poor her eyes were. As followers of Christ, she had informed me, we were to be modest and not bathe near other people, even though we were wearing our clothes. However, there were people close to the place where she had taken me to bathe and she hadn't even seen them.

To me there didn't seem to be any inconsistency between Sister Miriam's throwing away her contacts by faith and the fact that she couldn't see. I thought back to my folks and the pastor. With them, it was all talk about God having the power to heal. If they believed it, they certainly didn't act on their conviction. I had never seen them, or *anyone* in our congregation back home, throw away her glasses.

Impulsively, I decided that I wanted to be like Sister Miriam. I took out my contacts and threw them in the water. "I've done it, Sister Miriam," I called out to her. "I've thrown away my contacts, too."

She jumped to her feet excitedly. "Praise the Lord! Praise the Lord, Sister Rachel! Praise God!"

A warm feeling flooded over me. If God wanted me to see well, He would restore my sight. I was not going to depend on the crutches and wicked inventions of man.

6
The Gathering

I discovered that I had a great deal to learn before I was acceptable in the eyes of the rest of the group.

I had always thought the Christian life was one of fellowship and that believers were encouraged to share their joys and sorrows with each other. I soon learned, however, that Brother Evangelist had other convictions. The sisters took me in hand to help me adapt to camp life and an acceptable mode of conduct.

I talked too much, for one thing. "We sisters try to speak only when it is absolutely necessary," Sister Mary told me. "And we use as few words as possible. The Lord helps us to refrain from foolish words and vain babblings."

I honestly couldn't see how that applied to ordinary conversation, but I dared not challenge them. I had just come into the group from a sin-sick world. My own life had been steeped in deceit and evil. All of that had to be pushed aside if I were to be completely cleansed. To me, that meant following the teachings of Jesus as interpreted by the group.

"You use far too much carnality in your speaking," one of the brothers said. "Learn to praise the Lord at all times when you are talking."

As the instructions continued I began to understand why I had startled the brother so much when I offered him the apple.

"The sisters can be a snare to the brothers because of lust and the natural desires of the flesh," I was taught. "For that reason you are to keep your heads down when you approach the brothers, so they will not be tempted by looking directly into your faces. And you're not to speak to them unless they speak to you first, or unless it is very important, or you have a question to ask."

That night I lay in bed looking up at the canvas tent. It had been torn and sewn together crudely. I wondered if I would ever be able to live an acceptable Christian life according to the dictates of my new companions. I felt that my life was very much like that tattered tent. The tears were sins that I had been trying to eliminate in much the same way the sister who repaired the tent had done.

Jesus spoke of giving us new lives, but I was afraid mine wasn't very new or very acceptable. My personality had always been warm and outgoing. I had the ability to make friends and found pleasure in being with people, laughing and talking. I was sure the brothers, and at least some of the sisters, looked on me as frivolous and scatterbrained. Would I ever be able to live in such a way that I would be worthy of being called one of the blessed sisters?

Without the help of God I was sure I could not do it. Everything they taught about the Christian conduct of the sisters was foreign to me. Silently I prayed for the strength and wisdom to be like the others. They were so meek and godly that I envied them. I envied the way they had been able to accept the discipline of the group and longed to do likewise. Only then, I believed, would I be able to find true peace and happiness.

The brothers were patient with me and carefully went over the guidelines for a true Christian woman's life until I had learned them all and knew how to put them into practice. "You must be modest, truly humble and filled with love," they told me. "It is wicked for you to make yourself beautiful. . . ."

I didn't have to worry about that, I told myself, but I did have difficulty with the precept that the sisters shouldn't look nice. I had always enjoyed stylish clothes and liked to be attractive. Yet if this was not pleasing to God, I determined to put it aside. I was going to walk with Him, whatever the cost.

After I had been in camp for a week I was very concerned about my car and thought I should do something about it. By this time I knew that it might not be considered acceptable for me to approach one of the brothers, so I talked with Sister Mary first.

"Brother Evangelist makes all of those decisions," she told me.

I hesitated. I had heard that Jim Roberts (who called himself Brother Evangelist and was the organizer and leader of the group) was in camp but I had not yet seen him. "Would it be all right for me to go and talk to him?"

The brothers had carefully schooled me in the proper way to approach one of their number, but this was Brother Evangelist himself. Everyone looked on him with awe, as though he was only a step or two below Almighty God. I was terrified to think about talking to him. All day I prayed about it, asking God to help me speak to Erother Evangelist in such a way that I would not incur his displeasure. I didn't think I could stand it if he rebuked me.

Late in the afternoon I saw him standing alone near the camp fire. He was a gaunt, ascetic individual, taller than most. His burning eyes could pierce steel plating and he had a holy, other-worldly way. Even if he had not been pointed out to me I would have recognized him as someone apart from the others. There was a distant, unapproachable look about him. Had I not been so concerned I could never have gone over to talk to him.

He looked up as I drew near and I lowered my gaze, quickly. "I am sorry, Sir," I mumbled, "if this is being hasty, but I was wondering . . ."

"You were wondering about your car?" he interrupted, as though he had the ability to see into my mind and read my thoughts, even before I spoke them.

"Yes, Sir." I marveled that he knew what I was about to say.

"We have discussed the matter," he told me, "and have decided to send two brothers out to get it. They will probably sell it in Omaha. Praise God."

That was my first encounter with Brother Evangelist, and I was even more impressed by him than I had been before. Never had I spoken with anyone who seemed half so wise or half so holy. It was as though he knew all things and lived so close to God that he could not sin. It had bothered me when others in the group said "Praise God" in every other sentence, but when Brother Evangelist did it, I was thrilled.

I began to worry about his health. He had so many things to do around camp I didn't see how he could possibly keep up with his responsibilities without breaking physically. He was in charge of everything. He saw that the sewing was done and that the details were attended to. He arranged for Bible studies and instruction classes and handled all the problems that came up in the course of a day.

I admired him so much I soon found myself saying "Praise God" the same as he did. Only more often than not, I used the phrase when I didn't know what else to say.

When one of the brothers would bring me something to sew and explain how he wanted it done, I would automatically mumble, "Praise God." Afterward, as I thought about it, I realized that the way I had used the phrase hadn't meant a thing. That bothered me. But I was afraid to say anything about it to any of the sisters for fear of seeming worldly.

One day when Sister Mary and I were preparing the morning meal we confided in each other. "There is something that is bothering me lately, Sister," I said softly, so I would not be overheard. "I say 'Praise God' so much that there are times when I wonder if I really mean it." I eyed her a bit apprehensively, wondering if I had said something she would feel compelled to tell Brother Evangelist. But she agreed with me.

"I've thought about that, too. It doesn't seem right that we should say 'Praise God' all the time."

As we worked she continued, telling me that it even disturbed her the way the brothers used the phrase. "They will say something like, 'We need to get out of this world, Praise God, and really start doing what the Lord wants us to, Praise God . . .' They just stick the phrase in anywhere."

In that moment a bond was forged between us that strengthened as the days and weeks passed. I had always been the sort of person who had to have at least one close friend. I thanked God for Sister Mary. I could confide in her when I was troubled or lonely.

We were still in Iowa City when I became so concerned about my parents that I wrote to them. I slipped away from the other sisters, opened my Bible so it would appear that I was studying, and wrote to them, trying desperately to explain why I had joined the group. I wanted them to understand and approve, even though we were taught that our flesh people couldn't possibly grasp our reasoning. Tears filled my eyes and streamed down my cheeks as I wrote.

Dear Dad & Mom:

The Lord led two Christian brothers to Kearney and I feel the Lord led me to go with them and serve the Lord. . . . We go by no name . . . We dress modestly—the women in long skirts and smocks and the men in long robes hand-sewn by the women . . . The Lord provides us with food. We travel all over to speak to souls of the Lord. . . . You must understand I didn't have to go and that I could leave now if I wanted.

With love and prayers,
Rachel

Although I wrote this letter in Iowa, the brothers read it, taped it shut, and mailed it from Missouri so my parents wouldn't look for me in Iowa City.

A few months later I wrote them again, this time from California:

> . . . It is really a blessing to live separated from the world. I don't feel I can or should explain everything to you. I just pray the Lord will start to open your eyes to the way the world is falling . . . Christians need to get out of it.

In both letters I made myself believe that I was trying to share my faith with my parents. Despite my protestations of happiness and joy in the Lord, I feel now that in both letters I was reaching out to them, trying to bridge the gulf that I had forged between us and not quite knowing how.

September found us living on a farm near Fayetteville, Arkansas, where a kindly owner had given us permission to camp. It was a beautiful, peaceful place. The trees were already beginning to shed their summer green to don shades of fall. Although winter would soon be upon us, the birds hadn't yet begun to gather for the trip south, and the soothing quiet was broken only by their haunting melodies. I had listened to the birds on countless occasions in the past but it seemed to me that I had never before realized how lovely their singing was.

The nights were clear and sparkling with stars, and the warmth of the afternoon sun still lingered on the gentle slope where we had pitched our tents. I loved to take my sleeping bag and stretch it on the grass so I could look up at the shimmering sky. On those evenings I felt a oneness with God that I had never felt before. All seemed so perfect, so much in harmony with our Saviour.

I was sure, then, that I could spend the rest of my life with the group, doing exactly what Brother Evangelist expected of me. All the problems and confusion and turmoil I had left behind in Kearney, Nebraska were so far away that I could easily pretend they did not exist. The Rachel Martin who had lived there and dated Phil didn't seem to exist any more. Neither did the girl who lived only for nice clothes and the latest recordings and the approval of a bunch of worldly people. I had found a contentment I had never known before. There was purpose and meaning to my life.

From the very first contact with my new associates I had heard them speak of separation. They stressed the unquenchable joy available to anyone who was willing to sacrifice the things of the world and adopt the Christ-like existence that Brother Evangelist taught. I can't speak for the others, but I was happy at the farm.

Part of my contentment came from the fact that the owner of the land was sympathetic to our cause and gave us permission to stay there. Because we were on private property we were not hassled by the police or irate citizens who objected to our using public property.

Often our group was split up because of the pressure put on us by the authorities, but here we were together—all ninety of us. Brother Evangelist used the time to lecture us and strengthen us in the faith. I lived for those meetings. It seemed to me that I could have sat in his services around the clock, so precious they were to me.

None of the sisters spoke. It would have been a terrible sin for a woman to speak in public. Brother Evangelist or one of the elders always preached to us. I listened eagerly as they told of the selfless life we were expected to live. God wanted us to be unspotted before the world. Therefore it was good to deny ourselves for the sake of Jesus Christ. We were not supposed to yield to fleshly demands such as bathing, and eating between meals. Those things were weaknesses that did not mar the lives of the truly spiritual. Indulging in them was clearly a way in which we gave in to the flesh. We were encouraged to put off bathing as long as possible in order to demonstrate our spiritual depth and our lack of concern for the flesh. We had to learn to rise above such unimportant things.

I shall never forget the first time I heard Brother Evangelist speak. It was to be a big event and the entire camp was gripped with excitement. When I first joined the group he was so busy organizing travel schedules and handling other matters that the responsibility for speaking fell upon the elders. But now we were to be honored by a message from the great man himself. I heard about it that afternoon and was ecstatic. I could hardly wait until things were cleaned up from the evening meal.

I was deeply disturbed by the fact that I had to work that night. That was of Satan, I told myself. He was contriving to keep me from hearing the man of God who had the vision to lead us out from the wickedness of the world. But I was not going to allow the devil to keep me from hearing the Word of God. I worked frantically, thinking of nothing else.

When the time came for the group to gather, the caste system was most apparent. The single brothers took their places in the favored inner circle. Next to them came the brothers who were married, as though the act of matrimony placed them a little lower than the others. Behind the married men, their wives and children sat and the single sisters were left to find places on the outer fringe. Resentment flared as I saw the order of things within the group. I guess I had known it before but had chosen to ignore it. This was not what I had been taught at home about Christianity. Mother and Dad believed that God was no respecter of persons, that all were the same before Him.

Yet, I told myself, trying to follow their way had only brought me deep into sin. Now, I decided, I had found the truth through the teachings of the group and Brother Evangelist. They had brought me out of my sin into the purity of righteousness. My sudden, flashing anger must be still another phase of my carnality. It was the lust of the flesh to feel as I did about being assigned to a lowly position. My lack of spiritual discernment came because I did not properly understand God's teachings.

I was contrite as I took a place on the grass some distance from the others, asking God's forgiveness for my froward spirit. I wanted to be closer to the great man but felt my unworthiness so deeply that I remained apart from the group.

Everyone was caught up in the excitement of Brother Evangelist's appearance and the message he was about to bring. We all waited breathlessly.

At first I remained apart from the others, as though doing penance for my rebellious spirit. After a time, however, I was so anxious to be nearer that I moved, crowding in beside Sister Mary. She must have been as excited about the evening service as I was. She had taken a place as close to the married women as she could.

A hush akin to awe settled over the group as the gaunt, robed man stood to speak. Never before had he looked so magnificent to me—as holy as he did that night. He seemed even taller and more handsome than before. His flowing robe and neat beard and long rust-colored hair gave him a Christlike appearance. His deepset eyes seemed filled with love and concern for us. I could imagine him weeping over Iowa City or Chicago or Omaha, even as our Lord wept over Jerusalem. I thought my heart would burst with sadness. Cringing in my own sordid inferiority, I felt as though I wanted to fall on my face at his feet and worship him.

It seemed to me as though everyone sat a little taller than before. I found myself lamenting the fact that I could not stand up to get a better look at him. But I knew that would never do. Brother Evangelist highly disapproved of women being forward and making themselves conspicuous. Especially the single sisters. I thought of Zacchaeus who wanted to see Christ so badly that he climbed a tree. I was short like he was, but I lacked his courage.

Brother Evangelist did not begin immediately. He turned with deliberation, his piercing gaze fixed on one small area and then another. Only after he had surveyed everyone did he begin. I listened, awestricken. It seemed to me that it was actually God speaking through him.

"We have been called a cult," he began, "but we are not! We represent the true Christ. All others are imitations, or worse—representatives of Satan. The Moonies, Hare Krishnas, the Children of God and all the rest do not offer peace and salvation through Jesus Christ. Their followers are bound in sin."

I was to learn much later from a newspaper clipping in my father's files that Brother Evangelist had actually started our group five years before. His father had been a minister in West Virginia, and he apparently had been in a cult called The Process, which worshiped both Satan and God. But he said nothing about his background as he continued, explaining the differences between our group and the cults.

Then he turned our thoughts toward the Christian church. "Carnality is the curse of the Christian church today," he began, his voice a silver bell. "As you travel from place to place, preaching the warnings of Christ and the wrath to come, what do you see? Materialism and carnality on every side.

"Look at the churches that have been built in every town and city in America—great monuments to the pride of men and the love of the world. So-called Christians are more concerned about the pleasures and comforts of this world than they are the kingdom of God."

He quoted one portion of Scripture after another to

prove that we are in the last days and that the wrath of God was soon to be poured out on an uncaring world. I trembled as he thundered of the impending doom—thankful that I was to be spared, but terribly concerned about my family. Brother Evangelist was convinced that all our flesh people were bound for Hell, but I could not believe that about my own family. And I was sure that if he knew them as I did, he would not believe it, either. Jesus Christ had always taken first place in their lives. They had never been carnal and materialistic the way Brother Evangelist insisted they were. No one would make me believe that they would not be caught up with Christ when He returned.

Yet, I was disturbed by the fact that this one who seemed to be so very close to God could be so firm in his conviction that my flesh family was lost. I wanted to talk to him, to protest that what he said about my parents and sisters and brother was not true. But there was no opportunity for me to speak. Even if I had been given the chance to say what I believed, I would have remained mute—my own personality was crushed by the sheer domination of Brother Evangelist's personality.

While my thoughts wandered, Brother Evangelist had finished with carnality and had transferred his attention to our past lives. " . . . We should not think about the past," he ordered. "We should not talk about the past or we will be in danger of being snared by Satan. We will be like Lot's wife, unfit to escape destruction."

I cringed as I thought of the letter I had written to my parents and had mailed so furtively. Did this make me guilty of looking back?

The speaker continued and I dragged my thoughts, forcibly, from my indiscretion.

"What, then, should we do?" Brother Evangelist went on. "Speak only about the present and the future. If we must concern ourselves with the past, mention it only to illustrate the awful wickedness the Lord has delivered you from ."

I leaned forward intently, captivated by the gripping cadence of his voice that indelibly printed his words in my heart and mind. How long he spoke I do not know, but this I remember well: A certain sorrow passed over me—a shadow darkening my soul, as he finished and dismissed us with a word of prayer. It was as though I had been in the very presence of God and was now being sent away. A vague uneasiness took hold of me—a feeling of guilt that my banishment was caused by something I had done. But I did not know what it was.

Gradually my uneasiness fled, giving way to a peace I did not think I had ever felt before. How thankful I was that I had met the brothers in Kearney, Nebraska. Had that only been two weeks ago? It must have been a year—two years ago—a generation. I felt as though I had always been with the group, basking in the warmth of God's love.

Even my parents and family seemed far away and almost unimportant. God had sent the brothers to me that fateful night to rescue me from the slimy clutches of sin. How thankful I should be that I, of all people, had been rescued from the Evil One.

As I climbed into my sleeping bag that night, my mind pulled thoughts and phrases from the message I had just heard. The message Brother Evangelist had just given was surely the most wonderful, the most challenging anyone had ever listened to. I marveled at God's timing to send the followers of this holy man into my life when I was so far from the Lord. At the moment I was convinced that every word he uttered was holy writ, except for his charges against my family.

And I had an explanation—a quick excuse for that. Most of the flesh people belonging to members of the group were undoubtedly like he said they were, I reasoned. They would have to be, or one of his wisdom and discernment would not make such a charge. It was understandable that he would assume my family to be the same, because he didn't know them.

I went to sleep thanking God for the privilege of being with the group and under the teaching of Brother Evangelist. I didn't see how I could be so blessed. I, who had been so deep in sin.

Music was an important part of our lives. As sisters we were taught to be quiet at gatherings, but we were allowed, even encouraged, to sing.

Back home I had found singing the most enjoyable part of any church service. I have a fairly good voice and looked forward to being in the choir and smaller singing groups, even when I was living far from God. Now singing meant more to me than ever before.

The hymns the group sang were somewhat different from those I was used to. We sang a few very old songs, but most were considered part of the trappings of a decadent religion by Brother Evangelist and the elders. So we sang psalms set to music, and they were beautiful.

I quickly discovered that even with my limited knowledge of song writing and music I could compose scores for my favorite passages.

I had to be careful not to show excitement or joy, however, since modesty and a contrite heart were the badges of spirituality for the sisters. To have shown pleasure in an accomplishment would have been gross sin. Just having the feeling of pride was enough to make guilt well within me and often I would plead with God for forgiveness. It seemed that I would never reach the plane of spiritual maturity that marked the lives of the other sisters. Regardless of what I did, I was so very far from being what I should have been.

It was during this period of my life that I best remember our singing with outstretched arms. We were blending our voices in that lovely chorus, "Let's just praise the Lord. Praise the Lord. Let's just lift our hands toward Heaven and praise the Lord." We had never sung more sincerely, or more beautifully, as we praised God with our hands stretched heavenward.

ESCAPE

As I stood with the others in the gathering I thought about my friends at Nebraska Christian High School. Many times I had sat in chapel as we sang that chorus, while our hands were in our laps. As we sang the song that evening on the hill in Arkansas, the way we had sung it back at school seemed almost a mockery. But that was not surprising. During my high school years I had chafed under the structure of the established church and had become convinced that the brand of Christianity I saw exhibited there was chiefly a handful of do's and don'ts.

I remember how badly I had wanted to lift my hands in praise to God as we sang in chapel at school, but I hadn't dared. I was afraid of what the others would think. Now, as I felt the warmth of spirit, I longed for them to know the same joy I had.

I longed to go back to the high school campus with my new brothers and sisters in the Lord and tell those poor, misguided students and faculty what they were missing. I was sure that we had the truth and everyone else was following an illusion, a feeble carbon of what God had done for His children. They were unwitting pawns of Satan, lulled to peacefulness by the wiles of the Wicked One.

From thinking about our singing as a group when I was a child, my mind wandered once more to my parents. I tried to imagine what they were doing and wondered if they missed me as much as I missed them. Tears came to my eyes as I stood there, and again after I had gone to bed. I missed them deeply.

But I had forsaken that life, I tried to make myself believe. I had turned my back on my flesh people and the wicked things they were supposed to be involved with. But if it was God's will that I desert my blood-parents, why couldn't I stop thinking about them? Why couldn't I forget them? I buried my head in my pillow to keep the sister who was sleeping beside me from hearing my sobs.

I didn't say anything to anyone about the battle that

raged within me. I knew they would say that my concern for my flesh family was the result of carnality—that I was actually unwilling to forsake all to follow Christ. At times guilt all but overwhelmed me and I prayed for forgiveness and God's help in putting my own flesh people aside the way the others had done. Occasionally I was quite sure I could manage, but the comfort would only be for a little while. Then my loneliness and concern would come creeping back, and I was sure that I would *never* be able to love God the way I should.

7
The Accident

The days we spent on the farm were among the most enjoyable in the entire nineteen months I was with the group. In return for a little work, the farmer gave us access to his garden and we ate well. We sisters took turns preparing the meals in the two huge pots we carried with us.

Our diet varied little. We usually had a gigantic vegetable stew made of whatever was available. One day it might be beets and beans and peas with a few potatoes thrown in. The next it might have okra and onions or sweet corn or cauliflower. If we had flour, it would be added for thickening.

At home my mother planned all the meals, but in the group the brothers planned everything. We sisters waited for them to tell us what to do and how to do it. They even directed us in the kind of vegetables to serve at a given meal and how we should prepare them. The women had no decisions to make about anything.

I enjoyed that. When I had been making the plans for my life I had succeeded only in messing things up. It was reassuring to have someone tell me what to do. Since the brothers were so holy and so wise I was sure that I would refrain from sin if only I followed their orders. So I waited patiently to have every move directed.

I didn't even have to decide whether I should take a bath. If I felt the need to bathe, I was to ask one of the brothers. I would approach him quietly, with my head bowed and my hair pulled down over my face, in a proper state of subjection and humility. "Excuse me, Brother."

"Yes, Sister."

"Lord willing, would it be possible for this soul to take a bath today?"

"I will see about it, Sister, and let you know later, Lord willing."

"Thank you, Sir. Praise God."

An hour or so later he would call me from the sisters' area and inform me that God had provided an answer to my request. "Sister Rachel, Lord willing, it would be all right for you to take a shower about three this afternoon."

I didn't even have to decide what to wear when I got up in the morning. I had two outfits. I wore one while I laundered the other.

When we went witnessing the brothers told us who we were to go with, where we were to go and how long we should be gone. When we went on the road we were assigned to travel with a brother who did all the decision-making for both. We sisters didn't have to plan anything, and at the time, I liked that. It made life so much simpler.

Everything was so enjoyable at the farm that we hoped Brother Evangelist would allow us to remain there a long while. We would have liked to have stayed forever, but we knew that would not be possible. Our leaders did not believe that a true Christian should stay in one place permanently. We had to be out on the road, traveling from town to town, telling others about Jesus Christ and showing them the errors of their ways. Brother Jim Roberts had gone on, but we knew he was directing our activities and had left orders with the elders as to when we were to move and where we would go. Either that or he would join us at a time when we least expected him, telling us to pack and get out on the road again.

I had almost forgotten what it was like to have the filth of the road on my clothes and body. I could dimly remember how it felt to travel long distances—the terrible weariness and strain that always came over me when we were on the road for any length of time. It sapped my strength until I moved as in a trance, carrying on only because I had to.

I would have denied that I felt any of those things when we were hitchhiking about the country. To have admitted such a concern about human comfort was to admit to carnality and denial of our Lord. Brother Evangelist and the elders would have been unhappy with me had they known, so I forced such evil thoughts out of mind, trying desperately to deny their existence, even to myself. I dared not mention to Sister Mary or any of the others how I felt. I was sure, however, that they had the same desire I had. It was so enjoyable on the farm that I know they would have preferred to spend the fall and winter there.

But that was not to be.

Our quiet, peaceful interlude was shattered one idyllic September morning when the sun was smiling on us and the warm, late summer breeze was so gentle and placid it did not seem possible that the weather could ever turn cold and disagreeable.

The tragedy might never have happened had the farmer not been kind to us. He occasionally loaned us his truck to go to town for supplies. On that particular morning the elders had made arrangements to use the truck. One of the married brothers, Brother Lazarus, along with his wife and tiny daughter, got into the cab. Then thirty or thirty-five of us clambered onto the flatbed. We hadn't been to town since we reached the farm and were excitedly looking forward to it.

To have looked forward to going to town because of boredom and the desire for change would have been a sin, but not for the purpose of witnessing. We were supposed to get our happiness from serving the Lord to the exclusion of all else. That was what we talked about as we climbed on the truck and Brother Lazarus pulled out of the yard.

We weren't as hypocritical as it may seem. We were deeply concerned about sharing our faith with those less fortunate, who had never been privileged to hear the truth as expounded by Brother Evangelist. We were convinced they were all going to a Christless eternity in Hell unless we brought the gospel according to our leader to them. For all our concern, however, we had to adopt a pose of spiritual perfection to avoid censure by the elders.

At an intersection several miles from the farm, a motorcycle roared onto the highway from a side road directly in front of the truck. We heard the roar of his machine and saw it explode into view. At almost the same instant Brother Lazarus veered sharply in a frantic effort to avoid hitting him.

The truck careened wildly along the lip of the deep ditch. Then, when it seemed we were sure to go over, Brother Lazarus managed to whip the heavily loaded vehicle away from certain disaster. But only for a moment. We veered across the road to the opposite ditch where we teetered precariously fifty yards or so, then we lurched again to the other side of the road. Sister Mary and I screamed. A wild prayer for God's protection escaped our lips and mingled with our terror-stricken screams. By this time Brother Lazarus had completely lost control. The truck clung to the edge of the road bed for a hundred more yards, as though suspended by some invisible force, and then the law of gravity asserted itself and the heavily loaded vehicle edged onto the steep slope and rolled over into the ditch.

Brothers and sisters were thrown everywhere.

I don't know how long it was until I got to my feet. It must not have been long. I realized, almost immediately, that I was only bruised and shaken up. I could thank God that I had not been hurt.

For the space of a minute or more there was little sound from anyone. It was as though I was dreaming, or watching television with the sound off. Then one or two began to moan softly. The brothers who were uninjured began to move from one to another, checking to see who was hurt and how seriously.

I started to do the same when I remembered the teaching that the sisters were not to touch the brothers. It was as though we were lesser beings, while they were holy. I knew that even in a time like this the taboo had to be honored. If Brother Evangelist were there he would say that it should be, especially at a time like this. He would take the accident as the testing of the Lord—that God had permitted it to happen to see whether we would keep His laws in times of stress.

Some of our group had minor cuts and bruises, like those I suffered, while a few were more seriously injured. One of the brothers had a broken arm. The elders set the bone and prayed over him. I was wandering around aimlessly. I had never felt more helpless or bewildered in my life, wanting to help, but knowing I couldn't.

It was then that I saw Sister Marian, Brother Lazarus' wife. She was sitting apart from the others on the grassy slope, holding in her lap the bleeding body of her little girl. The child's right temple was swollen and turning a purplish blue. She lay motionless in her mother's arms, whimpering softly, like a puppy or a kitten that has been badly hurt. Tears streamed down Sister Marian's face. In some small measure I knew the agony she must be experiencing.

I felt my own eyes moisten and started to move toward her, but Sister Mary placed a restraining hand on my arm. "No, Sister Rachel," she murmured softly. "The brothers will take care of her." I turned to see that her face was white and drawn and her lips trembling.

While we remained motionless, staring at each other, we heard an approaching siren. The rescue unit! Praise God! Help was coming! Now Sister Marian's little girl would have medical attention.

One of the brothers took the baby from her mother, tenderly, and laid her on the ground. By that time the men in the emergency unit had piled out of the vehicle and rushed over to where our people were lying or sitting. One of the elders stepped in front of them. They stopped uncertainly, looking beyond him to the baby lying on the grass. She was coughing blood and a thin trickle oozed from the corner of her mouth.

"Can we help?" one of the crew asked anxiously.

"Thank you, no," the elder informed him. "We take care of our own."

As if he hadn't heard, another from the rescue unit knelt and reached into his medical bag. I waited hopefully, but the elder would not allow him to come close to the badly injured little girl.

"We don't need any of your help," he repeated firmly.

"But —"

"Our health is in the hands of the Lord. He teaches us to pray for those of our number who have physical needs. He will answer our prayers, if it is His will."

Frustration clouded the young medic's eyes and he stared helplessly at our self-appointed spokesman.

"This child has to have medical attention right away," he protested.

I was concerned that they would not allow the medical people to look at the injured girl. I not only had a brother who was in medical school, but I knew, first hand, what the profession could do. When I was five years old I had broken my elbow and the local doctor had placed it in traction. A year later I broke my wrist on the same arm and a different doctor took care of me. I was able to use my elbow so well the second doctor had trouble believing that my arm had actually been broken.

But the brothers were immovable. We appreciated their offers of help, they acknowledged, but we could not accept. That would be turning our backs on God and on our assurance that He would take care of us. The men of the emergency unit were staggered by our refusal of their assistance. They milled about helplessly, muttering profanely about our stupidity and at our God who caused us to be so ignorant.

While this was taking place a reporter for the local paper arrived and began to take pictures. Most of the brothers and sisters were so dazed by the tragedy they scarcely noticed him. I, among them. But two or three of the men realized the sinfulness of photography. They recalled Brother Evangelist's teaching against having graven images and raised their hands to shield their faces. None of us were aware at the time that those pictures and the accompanying story would be spread across the country, or that they would result in several of our number being restored with their families, even though we later fled the farm as quickly as possible.

At that moment the elders and the other brothers were so disturbed by what had happened and by the pressure of the rescue team to at least allow them to treat the baby that they were aware of little else. The doctor who had accompanied the unit was livid with rage.

"That baby is critically injured!" he exploded. "If you don't allow us to take her to the hospital immediately, we will charge you with manslaughter for denying her medical care."

But the brothers were adamant. "We are more afraid of breaking the laws of God," they said, "than the laws of man. If God wants the baby to live, she will live. If He is going to take her home to be with Him, you cannot stop Him with all your knowledge and your fancy hospital!"

When anger failed, the doctor tried reasoning, but that was no more successful. The impasse ended suddenly with a low wail from Sister Marian, the baby's mother. "She's dead! SHE'S DEAD!"

Furious, the doctor insisted on taking the body to town for an autopsy. The brothers were also opposed to that, but agreed reluctantly under threat of serious legal action.

Back at the farm once more, we huddled in small groups, crushed by the awful thing that had happened. In one terrible instant our world had been shattered.

Brother Evangelist had been firm in instructing us that we were to praise the Lord in all things. How could I praise God for what had just happened? How could I ever praise Him again?

Everywhere I looked I could see Sister Marian and her little girl. They were in the leaves of the trees overhead; in the clouds that scudded ominously over the darkening sky; in the numb, ashen faces of my silent companions. And when I closed my eyes they were also there—white, drawn features deeply etched in my mind.

If God loved us, why would He allow such a terrible thing to happen? And to a sweet, innocent baby? Sister Marian and her husband were among the most devout, most faithful in our group. Anyone who knew them could attest to their devotion—to their loyalty to God and to Jesus Christ. Why would something like this happen to them? Why? *Why? WHY?*

And why would something so awful happen to our group? We, alone, were serving God. We had forsaken our flesh people, our jobs, our comfortable homes and our cars to roam the country telling others about Jesus Christ. Why should this happen to us?

Then I got to thinking about the doctor and his anger at being refused permission to examine the baby. What would have happened had he and the other trained men been permitted to treat Sister Marian's child? Perhaps she would be alive now. Everyone was saying it had been God's will that the baby die, but doubt crept into my mind. Was it truly His will? Or was it because of the stubborn attitude of the brothers?

I had been taught to believe in the power of God to heal from the time I was old enough to talk. I had seen my parents kneeling to pray for God's healing hand on my brother or one of my older sisters, and when I was old enough to understand I knelt with them. But I had also been taught to trust the medical profession. Had God allowed the little one to die because of our adamant refusal to accept help? And, if Brother Evangelist's teachings were wrong about forsaking doctors and hospitals, in how many other areas of doctrine were they wrong?

A tiny crack appeared in my conviction that our group had divine revelation from God to guide us. It was invisible at the time, even to myself, but it was there. Time, loneliness, and the faithful Bible teaching of my parents when I was a child would widen it until I finally would see the truth.

But that night I was too tortured to think about it. I sat in silence before our tent, tears coursing down my cheeks. Brother Evangelist wandered about, also struck dumb by the tragedy. There was agony in his face and in the hunch of his shoulders and shuffling feet. Now and then he stopped to say a few words to a small group of brothers or sisters.

In spite of his subdued manner, I was still afraid of incurring his wrath. I didn't know what he would think about my crying and I hid it from him, lowering my head quickly as he approached. If he noticed, he said nothing.

I had cried from loneliness or disappointment or frustration on other occasions since joining the group. Now it seemed that the floodgates were opened, once I was in my bedroll or sitting up in the dark at night.

I cried a lot.

8
Cracks In The Armor

After the accident we tried to continue at the farm, but it was no use. The reporter who had covered the fatal incident ended our stay in the area and set us to traveling once more. The pictures and story he filed were picked up by the wire services and appeared in newspapers all across the country.

The flesh people of the brother who suffered the broken arm recognized his picture and came to Arkansas. By then he was flushed and feverish. His arm had been improperly set, causing infection which turned into gangrene. Over the protests of Brother Evangelist and the elders, he was taken to the hospital where massive doses of penicillin saved his life. As soon as he was able to travel, his family took him home.

Brother Evangelist was deeply troubled. He called us together and announced that we would have to leave at once.

"Satan caused that terrible accident in a desperate effort to crush the truth and keep us from sharing Christ with the people across America," he said. "He knows that we alone have the message that can save our country from the wrath to come. If we stay here, the publicity we have received will bring your flesh people descending on us and many of you will be lured into leaving—to your own damnation."

All the brothers agreed and we set to work quietly,

packing up and getting ready to leave. I did as I was told, meekly, and so did the other sisters.

We left the farm we had grown to love and took to the road in groups of two or three. I suppose the brothers knew where we were going and when we would meet again, but none of the sisters were told.

We met the others at a predetermined rendezvous near Dallas, Texas, before moving on to Austin where we spent a month or more. At first we were deeply concerned about the flesh people and deprogrammers. On that portion of the trip I learned that most of our moving around the country was not for the purpose of witnessing, as we had been led to believe, but to keep our whereabouts from those who might snatch some of our number from us and persuade them that we were wrong in our interpretation of the Word of God.

Losing disciples seemed to bother Brother Evangelist more than anything else. As the days passed without any indication that our location was known to our feared flesh people, we began to relax slightly and life for our group began to return to normal.

By this time I was known as Sister Charity. I had chosen my own group name and approached Brother Evangelist about it.

"Sister Charity?" He thought for a moment. "Sister Charity. That is what we will call you from now on."

I had selected that name because I longed to love and be loved—first by God, then by the brothers and sisters in the group. And finally, by those outside.

I particularly loved the children who traveled with us, and they seemed to love me. Being with them, however, brought an ache to my heart for my own nieces and nephews. They had held a special place with me from the time they were born. I liked to think I also had a special place with them. Closing my eyes, I could see them running toward me, their chubby arms outstretched, to clamber on my lap so I could tell them a story. How long had it been since I had seen them? Since I had even heard from them?

How I yearned to feel their soft cheeks next to mine. Tears rushed to my eyes as I wondered if they were sick and if they still remembered their Aunt Rachel. I had to lower my head quickly and look away to keep the brothers from seeing my hurt. I knew it was sin to look back, yet I could not help it, especially when it came to my sisters' little ones.

But there were the children in the group on whom I could lavish my love. That wasn't quite the same, but caring for them helped in a small way to ease the pain. So, when Brother Ted asked me to take my turn watching the children I was elated.

One of their number, a darling blond, blue-eyed eighteen-month-old little girl, captivated my heart. She was at the age when she was just realizing she could get the attention of everyone and found infinite delight in being the center of attention.

I was playing with her and having such a happy time, the other sisters began to watch. It was then that Brother Ted saw what was happening. He strode over to us, anger fierce in his eyes.

"Sisters!" he said coldly, "get back to work! This is just a baby! She is only flesh! Get your minds on the Lord!" With that he directed his disapproval at me. "Sister Charity, take the baby somewhere else and care for it. This is carnality! This is sin!"

His reprimand burned in my cheeks as I took the toddler away. Were the innocent antics of a darling little girl actually sin? I asked myself. I knew the brothers were much more versed in the Word of God than I, so what he said had to be true. But how could it be? I pondered long over that.

I was sure I loved Christ and wanted to walk with Him, regardless of the cost, but it was not easy to live up to the exacting standards Brother Evangelist and the elders set for us. We were constantly admonished to keep our minds on the Lord. Anything less was carnality and yielding to Satan.

We were also instructed that only those who have separated themselves from this present world and belonged to our group would be saved. At the twice-daily gatherings we had (when we were not traveling) Brother Evangelist spoke of the end time and the fact that judgment was soon to come.

"I must caution you again," he admonished, "to always be about the Lord's business, doing His will. You are also to pray without ceasing. That means constantly —every waking moment, even as you must always be in an attitude of praising God."

I cringed as his words thundered into my soul. We had been taught that he did not err when it came to interpreting the Scriptures and directing our activities. Although Brother Evangelist would have strongly denied it, we had our pope and were conditioned to accept his every word as the final authority.

As I was sewing, I was nagged by the thought that what I was doing was carnal, I should be reading my Bible. It was as though a great, oppressive hand was pushing down, holding me in subjection. I felt compelled to read the Bible. Not from love or a desire to learn, but from fear. I read because I was afraid of God's displeasure if I didn't. I went over chapter after chapter, reading words with a leaden mind. I was so numb and unresponsive I scarcely knew what I had read, but I was reading. I took comfort in that.

We were also told that we could not have possessions and still please God. We had to forsake all those worldly things Brother Evangelist and the elders had warned us against. We had to give up houses, cars, nice clothes—all products of our nation's manufacturing plants. They were evidence of man's rebellion against God and his attempt to be independent of God.

Mentally, I tallied our possessions. We had needles and thread, pencils and paper, candles and matches.

We wore ugly dark skirts and blouses with long sleeves and underclothing made of rough, inexpensive material. We also had one bowl and one spoon per person, and our tents, sleeping bags and backpacks. Obviously we had nothing that would be classified as possessions of value, so we could not have been considered materialistic.

My thoughts went back to my own possessions again, and especially to the pictures of my flesh family. I felt guilty about having the pictures. If any of the brothers learned about them I would have been reported to one of the elders or to Brother Evangelist immediately. Still, there was a tie with my family that even the group could not break.

At times I wondered if I had made the right decision and thought about leaving the group. I had no money but I knew my parents well enough to know that a phone call home would bring me an airline ticket. I would again be able to wear regular clothes and eat good food and sleep in a proper bed. Maybe, I reasoned during those periods of doubt, the group wasn't right after all. Maybe they were deceiving me.

But as soon as such thoughts came, I was convicted of them. *This is only the devil lying to me,* I thought, *trying to deceive me. I have to believe the Lord. Whatever questions I have He will answer in His own time. I must trust Him.* I bowed my head and asked His forgiveness for being so weak and worldly.

The topic of several gatherings centered on waiting for the Lord's guidance. I had many questions, and after each session I went up to one of the brothers as I had been instructed to do. Occasionally they tried to give me an answer, but more often than not they left me as frustrated and bewildered as before. "You need to wait on the Lord, Sister," they would tell me. "You must wait on the Lord in prayer. He will show you the answer when He wants you to have it." I didn't dare to voice the skepticism that crept into my mind at times. It seemed to me that the brothers fled behind that admonition when they didn't know the answers to my questions.

It was during this period that I decided to crucify the flesh in every way I could. It seems incredible to me now, but I felt then that one way to gain victory over the flesh was to put off going to the toilet as long as possible.

On one occasion I was in town with another sister, witnessing, when I stopped on the street in front of a service station. "Sister," I said, "I need to go in here and use the rest room. I am mentioning it to you because I know your mind is on the Lord. I have been putting off going to the toilet as long as I could, but I can't wait any longer."

She nodded. She understood my reluctance to use the rest room and the fact that I had reached the limit of self discipline.

As I got the key and went into the rest room I felt guilty that I had been unable to wait longer. To me, that was proof that I lacked the spiritual depth I should have had.

9
The
Tucson Incident

Although we had few problems in Texas with flesh people trying to snatch some of our group away, and though there were few difficulties with the Texas authorities, we did not remain there very long. Brother Evangelist ordered us to pack up and leave.

We straggled into Arizona and camped in the Molino Basin just off the Mt. Lemmon Highway near Tucson. Our campground was a beautiful spot where the warm days and refreshingly cool nights were a benediction.

There were several, in addition to myself, who were relatively new to the group and a great deal of time was devoted to indoctrinating us. We were eager to learn and were soon caught up in the philosophy and lifestyle of the group. We knew the reasons for shunning our flesh people and fleeing at the first indication any of them were in the area. I had no way of knowing whether anyone else felt as I did about their families, but we all gave outward evidence of accepting Brother Evangelist's edicts regarding parents and loved ones. We were as watchful as our leaders for evidence that our group might be being stalked by a family that could not accept the separation we demanded.

One of the brothers, a medical student, had joined us when we were camped in Iowa City where he had been going to school. We were all concerned about him. Brother Don had been married three years and his wife and parents would not accept the fact that he had chosen the Lord and our group ahead of them. They pursued us relentlessly.

I don't know how they were always able to learn where we were, but it seemed as though they had a pipeline to the very heart of the elders. It didn't matter whether we moved a few miles, across the state, or to another part of the country, eventually they would appear. On occasion it took them a little longer than usual, but we could count on the fact that they would find us. They did so repeatedly. No one knew how many times the brothers had managed to spirit him away just before his flesh people would descend on us with the sheriff and the terrible court order that could take him from us. It was a bitter ordeal for everyone.

We sisters were not supposed to know anything about it, but there were few secrets in our group. People talked and others listened. We knew what was going on almost as soon as the brothers did.

Sister Anna overheard some of the men talking with Brother Don. "I can't understand why my wife can't understand that I have made my choice and leave me alone," Brother Don said. "I left her a note telling her that I loved her but that I love the Lord more."

I thought a great deal about Brother Don and his problems and prayed frequently for him. We all did. The brothers had warned us repeatedly about this sort of thing. They had told us there would be testings as Satan stirred up our flesh people to try to locate us and snatch us out of our lives of peace and tranquility for the sure destruction of Hell. Would he be strong enough to resist this snare? That was the theme of our prayers on his behalf.

We all knew that Brother Don's flesh people were going to catch up to him one day. In a way we were resigned to it, although we were determined to keep him away from them. Still, we were quite unprepared for it when it happened.

We had been camped in the basin for some time. The authorities knew we were there. We had made no effort to hide from them, but there had been no hint of trouble. We had our gathering at the usual time that night, heard the same solemn warnings of impending doom for everyone save ourselves, and trooped off to our bedrolls. There were tents for most of the group but I was one of those who slept in the open.

I remember having difficulty getting to sleep that night. For some reason, I could not avoid thinking about my own flesh people. I wondered where they were, what they were doing and if they were out looking for me. When I finally went to sleep I slept so soundly that I didn't awaken until just before dawn the next morning, jarred to consciousness by a sudden squeal of brakes and the banging of car doors and the rough, harsh sound of male voices. Terrible, unreasoning fear seized me as I realized that it had happened. Brother Don's flesh people had come for him.

In reality, they had sent the authorities. It sounded like an army. I crawled out of my sleeping bag and pulled a blanket around my shoulders.

"Sister Charity," the sister next to me whispered, her voice trembling, "pray!"

I was already praying silently, huddled frightened and shivering in my blanket. The brothers had also heard the commotion. Brother Evangelist and two of the elders were up and facing the intruders.

"What do you want here?" our leader demanded. "We aren't breaking any law. What right do you have coming here this way?"

"We're looking for Don Harrison," the sheriff said coldly. "We know he's here so it won't do you any good to lie about it."

"We don't lie, praise God."

The officer ignored Brother Evangelist's indignant reply. "We demand that you turn him over to us!" He handed the leader of our group the writ from the judge that gave him the right to come into our camp and take one of our number away from us. There was a tense silence as Brother Evangelist slowly read the paper.

I shivered in the pre-dawn chill and looked around, as one in a dream. I was surprised to see a well-dressed man with a briefcase standing beside the sheriff. And scattered throughout our camp were deputies, revolvers heavy in their holsters, as though they expected the brothers to fight against them. I counted twenty-six of them, burly, hard-faced men who were ready for any kind of trouble. I remember thinking that they didn't know the brothers very well if they expected the sort of violence that would demand such a crowd of officers.

Brother Evangelist held the paper uncertainly and for a moment or two he did not speak, but when he did there was no indecision in his voice. "You have no right to come here this way!" he thundered, so defiantly we were all proud of him. "We camped here in the basin last year. You came out then and questioned us. We have never given you any trouble. This is harassment and is clearly an infringement of our rights."

There was a murmur of assent among the brothers, but the sheriff was not impressed. "You'll have your opportunity to tell that to a judge, if that's what you want. Right now we've come for Don Harrison. Where is he?"

I glanced furtively in the direction of a cluster of brothers standing in a little draw between our tents and theirs. There was no way Brother Don could have escaped. The authorities had moved in so quickly and in such force that one of those ugly, broad-shouldered deputies would have grabbed him before he ran ten feet. So the brothers gathered about, hiding him as best they could with their own bodies.

One of the deputies had been questioning the male members of our group while the sheriff confronted Brother Evangelist. "He's not here!" the deputy exclaimed. "I don't know how they did it, but somehow they got him out of here right under our noses."

The sheriff gestured in the direction of several deputies and they scattered to question other members of the group. I sighed my relief and silently thanked God for protecting Brother Don. For the moment, he was safe. But for how long?

I was so upset by what was going on that I was startled when one of the officers approached me. "Your name?" he asked.

I heard him but his words didn't register with me. It was as though he had spoken in some foreign language.

"What's your name, Miss?" he repeated.

"Rachel Martin," I answered. Brother Evangelist had told us to avoid giving our names if we could, but that we were not to lie. The deputy added my name to the growing list in his notebook.

While he did so I cast a quick glance toward the brother the authorities had come to get. I knew I shouldn't but I couldn't help it. I had to see if he was all right. *Brother Don is so sincere.* I prayed silently. *And he loves You so much. Protect him, God. It would be so awful if they find him and take him back.*

I almost gasped as I watched the deputy start in the direction of the small group that had gathered around Brother Don. I was afraid that my glance had given him away and remorse and fear overwhelmed me. But he had turned his attention to another one of our group. "Are you Richard Grainger?"

The brother nodded wordlessly.

"The sheriff wants to talk to you. Come with me."

By this time a second attorney had appeared with the inevitable briefcase in his hand. He extracted a piece of paper from it and handed it to the sheriff.

"Are you Richard Grainger?" the officer asked, repeating the same question the deputy had formed a moment or two before.

"Yes, I am."

"You're under arrest."

Brother Richard was stunned. "What for?"

"Suspicion of auto theft."

Our brother's forehead crinkled and he was even more bewildered than before. "There's got to be some mistake."

"The car you took when you ran off with this outfit was registered to your father and he has pressed charges. You're under arrest." The sheriff motioned to the deputy. "Read him his rights and take him in."

It looked as though the officers were about to leave. While I was disturbed about the fact that Brother Richard was being taken to jail I was praising God that He had protected Brother Don. I looked on it as a miracle. It seemed to me that God had made him invisible to the officers. He was right before them but they hadn't seen him.

Then, even that victory collapsed.

One of the two attorneys informed the sheriff that he had infiltrated our group not long before. "I spent two or three days with them," he said. "That was earlier this week. From what little I know of them and the way they operate I don't believe they would have had time to get Harrison out of here. Let's have another look."

The officers returned to questioning us one by one, finding out where we were from and noting our physical appearance in their records. The more they asked us the more terrified we became. Information such as they were getting would be invaluable to our flesh people in their searches for us. But there was no escaping. If we refused to answer we would be taken to jail and held until our identity was learned and verified.

While the others were being questioned Brother Don stood helplessly, looking on. Finally he was the only brother who had not been questioned. The instant the investigating officer turned to him, he recognized Brother Don from pictures his wife had given the authorities. He knew Brother Don even before he gave his name.

Our brother looked like a trapped animal. Fear, anger and resentment flared in his usually mild brown eyes. He was being taken captive so he could be returned to his hated flesh people. That wife of his was responsible for this, his eyes seemed to be saying. She had sent them after him. It was all her doing.

"What right did she have?" he asked aloud. "I'm where the Lord wants me to be . . . She says she loves me. If she really does, why won't she let me be here, happy, serving my Lord?"

I felt the fear and pain he was experiencing and my heart ached for him. The trouble was that flesh people did not understand this life of sacrifice.

Numbly we watched as the deputies returned in triumph to their cars and began to drive away. We were about to go back to our tents when the sheriff accosted Brother Evangelist once more. "Just a moment! I'm not finished with you yet. You've been accused of holding Mr. Harrison against his will."

"That's not true. Ask him."

The officer ignored our leader's protest of innocence, as though he hadn't spoken. "I'm not going to arrest anyone right now, but don't leave the Molino Basin until this matter is settled."

Brother Evangelist stared at him, tight-lipped and trembling.

"Is that clear?" the sheriff repeated.

Still there was no answer.

"I want your word that you'll stay at this campsite until I say you can leave."

"Lord willing, we'll be here," Brother Evangelist retorted grudgingly.

"If you aren't, we'll find you wherever you are and bring you back for trial."

"Our word is good. A Christian does not lie, praise God."

"You just see that you're here when I come out again."

When the sheriff joined the procession back to town

we gathered in little groups to pray for Brothers Don and Richard. My heart was hammering and tears blinded my eyes. I was more terrified than I had ever been in my life.

"What do you think will happen to them?" I whispered, as though I was fearful of being overheard. "Will they be taken to deprogrammers?"

Sister Mary nodded. "That's the first thing the flesh people will do to them now that they've got them."

I shuddered. We had been well schooled in the methods of the feared and hated deprogrammers. Once they got their hands on a brother or sister they wouldn't let go until the believer's faith was shattered. The deprogrammers would work in teams so they could keep the pressure on our poor, defenseless brothers night and day. They would not be allowed to eat or sleep or go to the bathroom and they'd be beaten severely until they recanted and rejected the group.

"Do you think they'll yield?" Sister Rebecca wanted to know.

That was even more disturbing than the thought that they would be subjected to torture and harassment. To turn one's back on the group was the worst sin a member could commit. It condemned one to eternal damnation. They would be lost forever.

For some reason, as I considered that possibility, I was thinking not of what would happen to our hapless brothers, but of myself. What if I were to reject the group? I had been privileged to become one of the chosen few—a member of the elect group who would be saved when God visited our tired, sin-torn world with destruction. I was unworthy. God knew the depth of my sin. He knew how I had deceived my family and Christian friends and associates. He had every reason to turn His back on me, but He loved me so much that He had made it possible for me to be saved. Me! I was terrified even to consider turning my back on these dear friends and fellow believers. To reject them would be the same as blasphemy.

We prayed during our stay in the Basin. How we prayed for our own brothers and ourselves, that God would protect us from our flesh people. For the first time, I had fear in my heart toward my own family.

Our experiences at Tucson brought a rash of newspaper reports. The account of the raid on our camp was highly publicized and individual reporters filed human interest stories. Tomas Gullen, a staff writer for the *Tucson Daily Citizen*, filed an account of the deputy who was sent to infiltrate our group a few days before the raid.

"I had a strange feeling, a feeling that my personality was being pulled out of me and being placed at his disposal. I felt afraid," explained an undercover deputy as he recounted how a religious cult 'alderman' tried to recruit him with mesmerism.

A bearded leader and the agent, Gary E. Martin, met nine days ago in Molino Basin, where Martin was sent to observe a group believed to be "psychologically kidnapping people."

"We sat down, and he just started quoting Scriptures. Then he gradually changed his voice to a soft monotone. I had to get close to him to hear him. As we talked on the ground near a spring, he started trying to catch my gaze. After three minutes of meeting his piercing yellowish-brown eyes I began to get a strange feeling. I felt afraid.

"I could feel his eyes reaching over and pulling," the forty-year-old deputy explained as his hands pulled off an imaginary pullover sweater.

". . . I came so close that I felt my personality rising out of my feet, but I escaped."

Martin said he escaped the grasp by not meeting the man's eyes, by not listening to the Biblical words coming out of his mouth and by forcing himself to think of other things.

"After about thirty minutes he gave up because he wasn't getting anywhere. He went back to why I was there. My cover story was that I had just gotten a divorce and had come up to read the Bible and get my head straight.

". . . the women didn't talk much to each other. One was humming a kind of religious hymn . . . and the children didn't play like regular kids. These little kids almost never spoke a word."

I asked God to keep my family from reading the story in the papers. I prayed that He would give us time to move on before any other flesh people appeared.

Brother Evangelist delegated two of the elders to attend the court hearing that Friday in late October. Mr. Grainger, Richard's father, was there. So was Brother Don's wife. They had had our fellow Christians examined by a psychologist and a psychiatrist.

Both men concluded that Brother Richard and Brother Don were unable to make decisions for themselves. For that reason Don was placed in the custody of his wife and Richard's father was made his temporary guardian. We took that to be a tool of Satan to get two of the faithful away from our group and into the clutches of their flesh people, but there had been nothing we could do to prevent it.

We were concerned that Brother Evangelist and the elders might be arrested themselves, and tried for holding Brother Don against his will. We were convinced that he had stayed with us because he wanted to, but we also were sure there was a conspiracy against us—that the courts and the authorities and their flesh people had joined forces to crush our helpless little group and prevent us from being saved when God destroyed the world.

I don't know how they managed, but the brothers learned the name of the deprogrammer who worked on

Brother Richard and Brother Don. He was from Ohio, they told us, and had been involved in deprogramming more than 500 from various groups. The following Saturday a press conference was held and we learned that the professional faith-destroyer, as we looked on him, had been helped in his task by two former members of our group. One was the brother who had broken his arm in the accident where the little girl was killed. The other was a sister whose flesh name was Allison Cordais.

Brother Evangelist had tears in his eyes as he related that information to us at our Saturday night gathering. "But we should not be surprised," he said. "Even Christ had Judas in his inner circle of apostles. Could we expect anything better than our Lord experienced?"

But with the disturbing information of the betrayal of our brothers, there was a faint glimmer of good news. The charges against our Brother Evangelist and the elders had been dropped now that the flesh people had received what they wanted. We were free to go.

"So," Brother Evangelist concluded, "we will be packing and leaving here immediately."

"Tonight?" one of the elders asked.

"Tonight. We have already lost five of our dear ones to their flesh people since we have been in Tucson. Satan is attacking in a way he has never attacked before. Who knows how many other flesh people have seen the publicity and are descending on us?"

Hurriedly we packed our gear and took to the road, two or three at a time, hitchhiking or driving in the few vehicles we had. Having the cars was really a contradiction to what we had been taught, but our beloved leader had told us that he had sought the will of the Lord in the matter and God had indicated that we should use them, but only for as long as He provided. Just what that meant, I did not know.

At the time I was not aware that the experience we had just gone through would be known as the "Tucson Incident" to parents with children in the group. It was the first time many of them had positive confirmation of where their children were, or that they were alive and well. I had no way of knowing that my own flesh brother, Tom, had seen the story in the *Omaha World-Herald* and associated it with the men I had been seen with in Kearney, Nebraska.

When Tom phoned my parents and read the article to them, Dad agreed with Tom's hunch. He phoned the attorney mentioned in the news account and learned that a girl who had identified herself as Rachel Martin was with the group. He also learned some things that convinced him to do whatever he could to get me out of the group. To have me living such a life of my own free will because I felt it was pleasing to God was one thing, Dad felt. But to have me roaming the country because of brainwashing was something else. And, according to the Associated Press story, a method closely akin to hypnosis had to be involved.

> . . . They isolate new members from all contact with the outside world, establishing a rigid new value system for them to memorize religious responses to any situation or question . . . When the two men taken from the group were asked their names they answered, "Cast not thy pearls before swine lest they rise up against you."

The attorney Dad talked with informed him that we had split into two groups. One had headed for Austin, Texas and the other for Oakland, California. The information was correct. I was in the latter.

10
The Arrest

Brother Evangelist had warned us that Satan would press for every advantage and use every means at his disposal to destroy our group. We were all desperately frightened as we left Arizona and the week that followed was torturous. Each town we approached, each state trooper we saw, was a threat to us and our walk with the Lord. Everywhere, there was danger of our flesh people attacking us and decimating our numbers.

And with good reason. The Tucson incident had blown the lid from our anonymity. Parents knew where we had been and where we were going. Even my own. Dad had been able to make contact with a Christian worker in the Iowa City area who knew a girl who had left us. She had been one of the former group members involved in the deprogramming of Brother Richard and Brother Don.

My folks got in touch with her and she phoned them later from Chicago saying that she and a friend were leaving immediately for California to meet with parents and attempt to get their children out of our group. She promised to learn what she could about me and get back to them. The following night she phoned again.

"One of the girls who knows Rachel well, Nikki Barker, was taken from the group and deprogrammed last night," Allison said. "But she doesn't know where Rachel is. She and three brothers left the camp a week ago to get food and hadn't returned. The others thought they had been grabbed by deprogrammers or had been arrested."

Actually, we had been arrested for sleeping in the park on a mountain slope near Berkeley, California. That mid-November morning one of the brothers wakened me while the dull gray mist of dawn was on the hills. I got up, shivering. It was my turn to help one of the married sisters prepare the morning meal. The married couples slept some distance away and we were to meet in another park to prepare the meal. As we started down the steep trail toward their camp the brother who was with me warned that it was slick.

"It rained during the night," he said. "Be careful where you step, Sister Charity."

The brother was several steps ahead of me, but neither of us was talking. I concentrated primarily on finding dry places to walk. Suddenly my companion stopped, raising his hand in warning for me to stay back. But it was too late. A police officer stood directly in front of us. He had seen us both.

"Pretty early to be out, isn't it?" he asked.

The brother remained silent.

"Been sleeping on the mountain?"

"Yes," the brother said. "We're missionaries and needed a place to sleep for the night, so we went up on the mountain." His answers were quick and I knew that he was hoping the officer would release us or move on down the mountain with us before anyone else woke up and blundered onto the scene. He was trying to phrase his replies to make the officer believe that only the two of us had been sleeping there. In that, he succeeded.

"You'll have to come down to the car so we can call in and check you out."

By this time the officer was joined by his partner. I was frightened when they handcuffed us and led us down the mountain. I knew what terrible things had happened in Tucson and wondered what was going to happen to me. I could envision all sorts of torture and harassment at the hands of the officers. I prayed that I would be able to resist the deprogrammers so I would not be eternally lost.

When we were almost to the bottom of the mountain a man ran across a field to the right of the trail. At first, fear leaped in my heart as I thought another of our number had been seen. Then I realized that the man was someone I had never seen before and was dressed in a way that indicated he was not a member of our group. One of the officers dashed after him and our bedraggled procession to the car increased by one.

"Officer," the young man who had just been caught said, "I might as well tell you now. You'll learn the truth soon enough. I'm out on probation. I've been looking for a job for several weeks but no one wants to hire me because of my record. I don't have any money and I had to have a place to stay, so I came out on the mountain. Can I go up and get my gear? I've got it stashed up there where I was sleeping."

One of the officers went back up the trail with him while the other took my companion and me down to the squad car. I was sitting in the back seat, confused and bewildered, when the radio crackled to life. It was the officer who had gone back, speaking on his walkie-talkie. "I've got two more of those robed men."

I looked miserably at the brother who was with me. Two more of our group had been taken by the enemy.

"Bring them down," the police officer in charge directed.

They called for another squad car and we were all taken in, arrested for sleeping on the mountain. As we pulled onto the highway I turned to the brother next to me and whispered, "Brother, what if we get separated? What do I do?"

"The reserve city is Portland, Oregon," he said quietly. "Go there as soon as possible." He saw my ashen cheeks and trembling lips. "The Lord will take care of you, Sister. Just trust Him and don't worry."

When we reached the jail I was separated from the brothers and taken to the women's ward, where I was fingerprinted and questioned. They went through my few belongings and put them in a sack. I was glad my pack was back at camp. At least they wouldn't be pawing through everything I had. As it was, I had little enough for them to catalog and keep for me. I had just cut out a coat from some insulated lining one of the brothers had found and I had that with me, planning to sew on it that morning after we had breakfast and the dishes were done. I was also carrying a purse. They took everything from me.

"Please, can't I have my Bible?" I asked.

"You can use a jail Bible," the matron retorted coldly. "Just ask for one when you want it. Someone will bring it to you."

It seemed to me that she softened a bit at that, but I was mistaken. She began to question me about drugs. Did I use them? Had I ever sold? Had I used marijuana? Heroin? LSD? It seemed incredible to her that I had not been involved in the drug traffic. She examined my arms carefully, expecting to find needle marks, and went back over the questions again. After what seemed like hours, she finally finished, then got up and walked over to where another matron was standing. I heard her say that she could get nothing out of me but she was sure I was on drugs. I couldn't have her thinking that about me, so I protested quietly.

The head matron came back to me immediately. "What did you say?"

"I don't believe the Lord would have me do such things."

"Did the Lord give you permission to break the law by sleeping on the mountain?"

I gave her the stock answer we were taught to use when asked about our living habits. "We are missionaries and we try to keep the law," I told her. "Usually we sleep in campgrounds. The Lord always provides places for us to sleep and we sincerely felt that the mountain was one of those places. We didn't realize that it was illegal to sleep there."

"Yes, of course," she mumbled sarcastically. With that, she took me to a cell in the felony tank. They still would not believe that I was not involved in drugs. At my request I was given a Bible to read and I sat on the edge of the hard cot, the Bible open on my lap. The words blurred before my eyes and I found myself reading the same few verses over and over again, unable to fully comprehend their meaning.

My family background rose to haunt me. I had always been taught to avoid breaking the law. I was probably the first and only member of our entire family who had ever been in jail. I tried to tell myself that I had been jailed because of my love for Jesus Christ, but that did little to help me accept, without guilt, the fact that I was now in jail.

It wasn't long until the matron reappeared and informed me that I was to go with her for my "mug shots," as she called them. The brothers had taught us that picture taking was vanity. Many times when we were witnessing we had bowed our heads or covered our faces quickly when cameras were directed our way. I was very upset. *What do I do now?* I asked myself. Then I remembered that Jesus had not fought when He was taken to trial. I decided I would not fight, either. As we left the room after the pictures were taken, the matron turned to me.

"You are entitled to one phone call."

I thanked her but declined. I couldn't call anyone in the group because there were no phones out on the hill where the others were camped. For one agonizing moment I was tempted to call my parents or someone in Kearney. I had no idea what was going to happen to me and was afraid to face the ordeal without someone at my side who knew me. Despite my determination to trust the Lord completely, I was terribly frightened.

Fortunately, I thought, the brothers had prepared me for such an eventuality. They had taught me that the devil would tempt me now in an effort to get me to talk to my flesh people. He wanted me to let them know where I was so they would come and get me and I would be lost forever. It would be weak—an awful sin to phone them.

"Are you sure you don't want to make a call to someone?" she repeated.

"No," I said. "I don't want to call anyone now." I thought I was being firm and decisive, but she must have realized my hesitation.

"I'll let you call tomorrow if you decide you want to."

I hurried down the hall.

It wasn't long after the matron had left that one of the other girls in the block loudly wanted to know what my name was. I had learned in the group that our names were not important. It was fleshly to be concerned about such things, so I sat quietly without answering.

But they would not give up. One after another pestered me with questions until I could stand it no longer. I answered only to get them to be quiet.

"My name is Rachel," I said with a quiet, meek voice. "I am in jail because society didn't like the way I was living. I have learned to live separated from the world. My friends and I were sleeping in a place God had provided. The law found us and said we weren't supposed to be there, so we were arrested."

I didn't look up, so I could not see the look on their faces. But I could tell they thought the new girl in cell number five was a real weirdo.

I felt dirty and unclean just listening to their vulgarities and profanity. One by one they boasted of the encounter with the law that had brought them there. One had been picked up for carrying a switchblade. Others were in on charges of possessing guns or drugs. They didn't talk directly to me any more that day, but at night one of them asked if I could sing. When she learned I could, she wanted me to sing a song for them.

I remembered my training of the past few months and politely declined. "I don't sing for people," I informed her. "I just sing for the Lord. But if you want to listen while I sing praises to Him, I won't mind."

That night I sang in that dismal cell block. So ended my first day in jail.

Early the next morning, after a sleepless night, the matron appeared once more and said I could talk to the public defender if I wanted to.

"What is a public defender?" I asked, "and what does he do?"

"He will represent you when you go to court. He might even be able to get you out of jail until the day of the trial without paying bond."

I was taken to a small room where a well-dressed young man was seated at a long table. He questioned me for some time but I refused to give him the answers he wanted. He asked my name, where my parents lived, and if they knew where I was. Finally I informed him that I didn't want to discuss my past life, even with him. "I forsook my flesh," I said, looking down to avoid his eyes. "My life now is living for Jesus and that is all I want to talk to you about."

"It would help me to know about your past."

"I'm sorry." I really wasn't, but it seemed to be the thing I should say.

"You would rather stay here, then?"

"If this is what the Lord wants."

"I don't think the Lord would want you in jail," he retorted angrily, closing his briefcase after jamming the paper inside.

"It doesn't matter to me," I said. "It isn't any better on the outside than it is in jail." I was parroting the words of Brother Evangelist and the elders.

The matron said something to him as he went by.

"No," he exclaimed loudly, "she just wants to stay in

jail and praise the Lord."

When I was taken to the cell outside the courtroom where we were waiting for our turns before the judge, the girls began to talk of their past lives. One was furious with her husband. "Here I am," she said angrily, "and that louse I married—the junky who made a junky out of me—is out on the street. He's a prostitute, too, but he was never able to sell himself for as much as I did. He's next to worthless."

Seeing the bitterness in her face and hearing from her own lips the sordid details of her messed-up life was almost more than I could take. I shivered, although the day was warm.

I was sitting quietly on the floor, listening to them talk and thinking that the Lord was far from them, when a young stranger looked over at me. "What's she in for?" she asked with a jerk of her finger in my direction.

"She doesn't talk all that much," one of the other girls replied, "but she's in here because she's religious. They were sleeping on some mountain and it was illegal. She claims that all she wants to do is serve the Lord."

"Hey, how come you're serving the Lord?" Now she turned and directed her question to me.

I tried to explain as I had been taught by the brothers. "I *had* to leave everything and show the Lord how much I loved Him. I even had to leave my flesh people—my parents."

They stared at me. "What about that verse that says you are to honor your father and your mother?" one of the girls demanded.

"I honor them," I said softly, "but I don't go along with what they believe."

As I was speaking I noticed a girl sitting in the corner of the cell. I had heard the others talking about her. She was supposed to go directly to the hospital from jail to be treated for depression and drug addiction. She had tried to commit suicide and had been put in solitary confinement. Someone must have mentioned to her that

I could sing, for she asked me to sing a song for her before she would be taken to the hospital.

I sang "Through It All," after making it plain to her that I was not singing to show what a beautiful voice I had.

When I finished singing I had an opportunity to talk personally with one of the girls. She told me that she had been in and out of girls' schools, reformatories, and jails.

"How can God help me?" she asked. "Will He help me get out of here?"

"I think He would," I said, "if you really prayed."

"The only time I ever read the Bible is when I get put in jail. Look, I'm sentenced to two years and I have a six-month-old baby." Her eyes filled with tears. "That's the hardest part—my baby."

I tried to put myself in her position. How could God help her? What could He do?

"Read your Bible," I suggested, "and really trust God. Pray that He will straighten out your life."

"I want to," she said, her determination growing. "I will!"

After that, my stay in jail didn't seem so bad. God had put me there for a purpose, I reasoned. He had me arrested so I could talk to this girl and help her see her need to trust Christ.

When I was taken back to my cell, I asked for my Bible again. It was never brought to me. And there was nothing else to do—that was the most difficult part. If they had just put me to work scrubbing floors or dusting or ironing or anything to keep my mind off my predicament, I would have found the stay much easier to take. All I could do was lie on my bunk and listen to the others talk. They had three subjects: food, drugs and sex. They discussed the food they craved, the trips they had taken on LSD, and talked for hours about sex. How thankful I was that I was able to talk to the Lord. It was the one thing that kept me from going out of my mind. As I tried to sleep, tears streamed silently down my cheeks.

The second day dragged on with the same endless inner aching. The authorities seemed in no hurry to process us and take us to court. Around noon the matron appeared and said it was time for us to go down to the holding cell once more.

I waited there until I heard the names of the brothers being called. I glanced up at the clock at the end of the hall. It was almost five in the afternoon. I knew what was coming next, and felt my body tense. When my name was called and I entered the courtroom, I was surprised to see that the judge was closing his books and preparing to leave. The afternoon before when I got a glimpse into the courtroom I saw that it had been filled with people. Now, it was almost empty.

The bailiff came over and told me the charges against us had been dropped. "You can get your things at the desk," he said. "You are free to leave. Your friends will meet you in the front office."

Confused, but thankful, I walked out of the courtroom, down the hall and out onto the street. As I stood there, savoring the sunlight, I thought, *I could just go now if I wanted to. I could leave and never see any of the group again. There's no one to stop me.*

But I couldn't do that! I wouldn't! It almost seemed sinful to have such a thought. Hadn't God protected me? I was in His will. I could not leave the brothers and sisters.

I stepped back into the building and went to the desk where I had already gone to pick up my own belongings. By this time the brothers were about ready to leave. Together we walked down the steps and out of the jail.

We walked back to the park where we had been meeting to eat, but nobody was there. It was seven o'clock in the evening. If the group was anywhere nearby, they would most likely be having a gathering.

"We'll have to go out and look for them," one of the brothers said, but without conviction that we would be able to find them. Once we had disappeared, Brother

Evangelist might have decided to move on. Our only hope of finding them was to walk the streets and pray that we would locate someone from the group out witnessing.

As we turned onto Telegraph Avenue, one of the busiest streets in the area, a red Mustang whirled around and stopped in a nearby parking lot, shining its lights on us. Suddenly the doors flung open and Brother Evangelist jumped out. We had a time of rejoicing there on the street.

The brothers had been driving around, trying to find out what had happened to us. They had no idea who had come and taken us, but were almost convinced that the deprogrammers had grabbed us.

That night I learned that Sister Nikki, one of my close friends, had been taken by the representatives of her flesh people.

Back home, when Dad and Mother found out that I had disappeared, they were deeply disturbed. One of the faculty at the college where Dad works had a brother on the police force in San Mateo, California. He offered to phone him and have him check the arrest records for that area. His report was encouraging in that they learned why I had disappeared. I had been arrested, they discovered, but had been released two days later.

At the end of the week Allison phoned them that I had been seen in the park. "If you come immediately, you might be able to locate her," she said.

The folks took the next flight to California, talked with Allison, Nikki and the others, and rented a car to drive around the streets of Berkeley to try to find some of us. At noon on Saturday they spotted some of the brothers and sisters and tried to follow them to locate the camp.

Word was out that we were again splitting for travel. We were supposed to be heading for Portland, and Mom and Dad wanted to get me before we left California. Who knew when they would be so close again? They finally thought they had located our camp but decided against trying to rush us. The terrain was too rough for them to move rapidly, and it would be hard to approach the camp without being heard or seen. And even harder to get me away if I didn't want to go with them.

They looked all day Sunday and finally saw three of our group. They asked the brothers about me, but of course that was useless. The brothers wouldn't give out information. Dad was confident, however, that they were soon going to find me and get me back, especially when they located the pack that Nikki identified as mine.

There was another encouraging piece of news for my folks. The father of one of the brothers who was arrested with me had come to California, gotten him released, and had taken him to a motel room to deprogram him.

My folks were allowed to go to the motel room where the brother was being held. They had an opportunity to talk to him and it became obvious to them that he had no idea where I was. Even if he was deprogrammed and anxious to help, there was nothing he could do.

By Monday my parents had exhausted all the leads they had. Disappointed, they returned to Denver, carrying the small homemade backpack that held my few possessions.

Dad looked at Mother. "I wish we hadn't taken this now," he said. "Rachel may need these things."

Mother started to cry.

11
"Through Our Suffering We Are Encouraged"

Something seemed to have happened to our group while I was in jail. Perhaps it had started earlier and I had not recognized it. Now, however, I began to see hints of jealousy and greed.

Having lost my pack, I had to borrow toilet articles from some of the sisters. That's when I first recognized the change. I had asked one of the more friendly sisters if I could borrow her hairbrush, and displeasure gleamed in her eyes.

That startled me. We were to share all possessions—to place no value on them at all. Although it was obvious she didn't want to, she got me the brush, but I was shaken by the experience.

As we prepared to leave California for the East, we were divided into small groups. Brother Evangelist was particularly careful now that Tucson and Berkeley had turned out so disastrously. Those of us who he suspected had the more aggressive flesh people, were sent in a boxcar. I was in that group. Although I knew nothing about it, Brother Evangelist had been well briefed on the appearance of my parents in California. He wanted to be sure that I was protected from them.

Riding in the boxcar was not an ordinary mode of travel for our group. The freight train was bumpy and since it was late November, the car was cold. I had no idea where, exactly, we were heading—just east. As the train rumbled on I began to think about my parents and the fact that Christmas would soon be upon us. Several times I asked the elder in our group if he thought we would ever go to Denver. What I was really wondering was whether, on this particular trip, we would go to the city where my parents lived, but I dared not ask so pointed a question.

"Do you think I could witness to my flesh people?" I asked him, hopefully.

He always gave me the same answer. In fact, it was the same answer I always received when I posed the question to any of the brothers: "I think you should wait on that, Sister. The Lord will work it out."

There were twelve of us in the boxcar. The train did go through Denver and it did stop. One of the sisters and two of the brothers got off. After they were gone, I wished I could have told her to phone my parents. I didn't want to leave the group. I didn't even want to give my folks any information that would help them find me. But this was the Christmas season. I knew they would be thinking as much about me as I was about them. They had shown me over and over again that they loved me, and they would want to know I was all right, even though they could not find me.

I wanted desperately to ask this of the sister. But I didn't.

I will never forget the look she gave me as she turned and studied my distraught features. She understood how I felt and wanted to help. Yet, she did not know what to do, or what I wanted her to do.

Just before she left I said, "If it were the Lord's will that I see my parents, I would be the one getting off. Since you are, it must not be what He wants." She heard me say that, but read the truth in my eyes. As soon as she had gone I wished that I had slipped her their names and phone number. But I had not, and the opportunity was gone, as quickly as it came.

The next day we rode through Nebraska. It was

snowing, as it often did there at that time of year, and I stood where I could see out the boxcar door. The miles passed slowly and at times the cold was nearly unbearable.

I was familiar with all of that area, remembering the name of the next town by the name of the one we were going through. If only I could stop the train and get off to phone my ex-roommate. I felt a sudden wave of concern for her. It was more than concern, but I didn't recognize it at the time. It was a deep loneliness and longing for my flesh people and the flesh friends I had left behind. We were finally getting back to the area where I had first joined the group. I couldn't help wondering where I would be living and what I would have been doing if I had not gone with the brothers that night so long ago.

At last we reached Lincoln, where one of the sisters and her husband got off. She had been having terrible headaches, and the constant rumble of the wheels and the jerking of the boxcar had made her miserable. But that was not the reason they left us, according to the explanation we were given.

"My husband and I have some friends here and in Omaha," she said. "The Lord has revealed to him that we should stop and witness to them."

I thought immediately of my flesh brother and his wife, Tom and Janell, who also lived in Omaha. How my heart ached to see them. *If it is the Lord's will,* I thought, *I will get sick and have to get off in Omaha.*

My left arm started to itch violently and I pushed up the sleeve of my heavy smock to look at the swollen, reddened flesh that was rough to the touch. I had mites, caught from sleeping next to a sister who had them. But such a minor inconvenience would never be considered great enough to allow me to leave the train. I was sure of that. According to Brother Evangelist, it was one of those torments of Satan that we, as believers, had to go through. Satan was trying to get us discouraged enough to be swayed from our purpose of witnessing for Christ. So I had to stay.

When the train stopped in Omaha it was all I could do to keep from bolting and running to the nearest phone to call Tom. But I realized, even as the thought came, that the brothers would never permit that. I was miserable during those few hours in Omaha, and for several days afterward.

If we were to give up our flesh people as though they had never existed, I reasoned, *why would my heart ache so much for them? Why wouldn't God give me peace that I was doing the right thing?* Although I could not allow anyone to see my tears, I was crying again as we crossed the Missouri River on our way east out of Omaha.

We were on the train for seven days, eating the little food we had brought with us, or having the brothers dash for the supermarket garbage cans in places where we were stopped a few hours. I did a great deal of thinking about our final destination and decided that we were heading for Washington, D.C. That was one of the places our group frequented occasionally.

I could not help thinking of the last visit I had made to our national capital. It had been only two weeks or so before I had joined the group. My sister and her husband, Jerry Regier, lived there, and I had visited their home. I knew where it was. Perhaps we wouldn't be too far from them.

I prayed that God would allow me to get out to their street or meet them somewhere. Jerry's work with Campus Crusade for Christ would take him around a lot. It wouldn't be too much to expect to see him, especially if we were in the same general area. Then I remembered a letter I had received from my parents just before I left Kearney with the group, and icy hands gripped my stomach. Jerry and Sharyn were thinking about moving and had been looking at a different house. If they had moved I wouldn't be able to find them.

I had been right about our final destination. We met

some of our number in Washington, D.C., but I soon realized that some of my closest friends among the sisters would not be joining us. The accident in Arkansas and the problems in Tucson and Oakland had caused Brother Evangelist to be much more cautious than before. He had decided that we must keep a lower profile. Since our group of ninety was now too large to travel together or to camp in one place, we had been divided into three groups. One group went to Wisconsin. I didn't learn where the second group went, but we were sent to Washington, D.C.

I was the first single sister to go to the nation's capital. On our arrival in the city we stayed under a concrete bridge. I found some city maps and hurriedly looked up the street where Jerry and Sharyn lived, noting how far I would have to go to get there. But that would be useless, I decided. They had most likely moved months before.

Camping in tents had caused trouble in California, so we looked for abandoned buildings to stay in, where we would not be in the public view. That was not as difficult as it would seem. Every city we visited was liberally sprinkled with empty houses and apartment buildings. Either the owner would be absent and not know of our moving in, or he would actually give us permission. We much preferred the latter since it kept us from having trouble.

Although I had no idea where to look for Jerry and Sharyn I continually searched for them every time I went out on the street. *Perhaps the Lord will allow me to run into them today,* I thought.

And on one occasion, while the sister and brother I was with were talking to people on the street I slipped into a phone booth and thumbed quickly through the book, hoping to find their phone number and street address. But they weren't listed. I don't know what I would have done had I found their number. I hadn't thought through the situation that far. But the old emptiness and aching came back as I realized that, as far as locating them was concerned, I had again come to a dead end.

We spent two weeks in Washington before moving on. They went all too fast for me. As I packed to leave I felt as though I was abandoning part of myself. *Why, God?* I asked silently. *Why didn't You permit me to find Jerry and Sharyn, or at least to get their phone number?* If I could just have dialed them and heard them answer, it would have helped to dispel the loneliness that enveloped me.

When the time came for me to leave for Florida I was assigned to travel with Brother Micah. He had been with Brother Evangelist for six or seven years and was one of the most trusted members of the group. When Brother Evangelist was not in camp Brother Micah, along with the other elder brothers who were with us, was given the responsibility of organizing camp duties and handling travel assignments.

Traveling with him was a totally new experience. Brother Evangelist had drilled us with the concept that unnecessary talking and laughing were frivolous and an indication that the flesh still had control. Brother Micah had no such inhibitions. We laughed and talked constantly. I found a blessed relief to be more like myself again. Brother Micah was a real Christian brother to me. Yet, a small nagging voice kept trying to convince me that it was wrong for me to enjoy myself.

We spent four days in Chapel Hill, North Carolina and a week in Athens, Georgia before going on to Florida. I will never forget the night we bedded down near the Interstate, twenty or thirty feet from each other. The constant rumble of the trucks made sleep virtually impossible. Finally I asked a question I would not have dared ask anyone else in the group. "Brother Micah, do you mind if I sing?"

His answer was quick. "That would be a lot better

than listening to those semis."

I was relaxed and comfortable with him. At least for most of the trip. By the time we neared the next camp he began to change, and when we got there he was totally different than he had been on the long trip.

The others had already eaten when we arrived, but because we had just come in off the road some of the sisters prepared food for us and we sat down to eat. It seemed as though Brother Micah had suddenly become a total stranger. Even though we were sitting across from each other, he said not one word to me. Nothing. And by his actions I knew better than to speak to him.

I am sure his attitude toward me had not changed, but his new manner devastated me. Just when I thought I had found a friend, the wall went up and he was a stern, solemn-faced brother again—the ideal example Brother Evangelist wanted him, as an elder, to be.

I thought about the other camps I had been in. At times, when Brother Evangelist wasn't there, it would get noisy and a little disorganized. Why couldn't it be that way all the time? Why couldn't our lives within the group be relaxed and cheerful?

I had been taught that God wanted His children to be happy, that He would approve of smiles and laughter. We were not supposed to live and act in a way that would be pleasing to Brother Evangelist or any other individual; we were supposed to do that which was pleasing in the sight of God. If He approved of laughter, why should our leader be so opposed to it?

That night as I lay in my bedroll, sobbing quietly over the sudden rejection by Brother Micah, I thought about Brother Evangelist and the rigid rules he had set down for us. We were not to show great concern each other. Such a display of emotion would be fleshly. The Bible taught that salvation was by grace. God's love had freed us from sin and the law. Yet, Brother Evangelist would have us carry the burden of his special list of regulations. We were not controlled by grace and love—we were ruled by fear, brought on by our confusion and the misleading of the devil. If that were true, then Brother Evangelist was wrong and my parents and pastor were right. But the leader of our dedicated little group was so sincere, so persuasive in his arguments. *What is right?* I asked myself. *Am I following a true disciple of God?* A chill swept over me.

I thought back to the marriage one of the girls had told me about. A brother had decided he wanted to marry one of the single sisters. They asked her if she wanted to marry him, and I'm sure she would not have been forced into the ceremony had she refused. The truth was, however, that we were so conditioned to accepting the word of the brothers as final that it is inconceivable she would have refused—regardless of her personal feelings. (I was thankful God had protected me from that sort of situation. I am afraid I might have done as they asked, even though I would not have wanted to.)

The brothers had the couple kneel and they knelt around them, praying for them. When they finished praying, the couple was pronounced married. No marriage license. No minister. No vows. How could they call such a union marriage? Yet I knew, even as the thought came, that Brother Evangelist would have given an explanation had I gone to him.

And when the ceremony was finished, the brother handed his bride a list of rules. She was to:

1. Never question anything he did or said.
2. Obey his every command immediately.
3. Make herself his servant, nothing more.
4. Eat only after he had eaten and had his fill.
5. Use "Sir" when addressing him.

I shuddered as I considered those demands. Would I be faced with the same sort of subjection when I married? If so, how could I be happy? Or should I expect to be?

My mind could not sort out the truth. What did the Bible mean by the admonition against carnality and vain babbling? Was enjoying life in the Lord a sin? How could it be? And why were women in such extreme subjection that we had to ask the men for permission to do anything? Why should we have to depend upon them for every decision? Hadn't God given us minds that He expected us to use? Had He created us as lesser creatures?

As I lay in my bedroll wrestling with my doubts and unanswered questions I realized that it was sinful to let myself get involved in such trivial things. I knew what Brother Evangelist would say if he knew of my concerns. He would scold me severely. I was letting Satan get the upper hand. It was sinful for me to even think such things. As a woman, I could not expect to understand. Brother Evangelist had faithfully taught us the true order of God's inner circle—the saved who made up our little group.

"The Lord has revealed things to me and the brothers, Sister Charity," he would have said coldly, "and we have passed that truth on to you and the rest of the sisters. These are special revelations for our faithful little band because we, alone, walk with God."

I could accept that, I told myself, if I could only get clear answers from the brothers when I asked a question. Instead, they would say, "Wait on the Lord, Sister!" That may have satisfied some of the young women in our group, but it only increased my questioning.

At last loneliness and depression gave way to a fitful, restless sleep. When I awakened the next morning I was as tired as I had been when I went to bed. Wearily I climbed out of my sleeping bag and looked around.

We were living in a long, narrow building that resembled an army barracks. There was one big room with smaller rooms on the sides, a kitchen and a bathroom. Across from the building I was in there was another that we were permitted to use. Attached to it was a large room that became our dining room.

The buildings were fairly clean but the room where we sisters slept had piles of leftover lumber stacked in it. The room was eventually to be a bathroom and there were three toilets along the wall that hadn't yet been installed. We were crowded into the rest of the space—wall to wall sisters. We had several mattresses and took turns sleeping on them. One of the sisters slept in a hammock strung from one corner of the room to another.

A new concern seemed to take hold of the brothers. One of them would come in every evening to tell each of us where to sleep that night. They were careful to keep shifting us around so we wouldn't form any close relationships with anyone else. I could not understand the spiritual basis for that, either, but I did not ask about it. Instead, I locked the question in my heart and pondered it at night when I was trying to get to sleep, or when I was somewhere alone.

Brother Evangelist gave the brothers permission to work in the fields as migrant workers. This, he was careful to inform us, was because they were not required to have social security cards. Fourteen or fifteen brothers went out to work each day for wages anywhere between a dime and a quarter a bushel. They were paid daily, which also pleased Brother Evangelist. According to him, that was the only scriptural basis for payment—a day's wages for a day's work. It also gave us the freedom to leave at a moment's notice, without having to go to anyone to be paid.

The brothers picked oranges, tomatoes, peppers and cucumbers and earned a fair amount of money—more than we had had in a long while. In addition, on some days they were even allowed to bring home some of the poorest produce in addition to their wages.

The rest of us spent our days cooking, washing, cleaning, witnessing, and studying our Bibles. One night Brother Evangelist announced at the end of the meal that any of us who had unpaid bills from the world should see him after the gathering. Money was coming in and it was time to take care of our debts in accord with the Scriptures that say we should not owe any man anything. I told him about my unpaid doctor and phone bills. He wrote them down and paid them.

It was obvious to me that we were going to be leaving Florida soon. There was new activity among the brothers and word began to leak down to us to get ready to move. Again, we were to go a few at a time and by different routes, in order to attract as little attention as possible.

It was during this period that the mite bites on my body began to irritate more and more. One morning Sister Phoebe noticed that her bites had become infected. She was miserable, and I wondered if I would have infection in the sores on my hands, too. It wasn't long until I knew—just a few days later, the skin around the sores reddened, and they were filled with pus.

At first I shrugged them off as a minor irritation, but soon realized that they were more than that. The pus caused pressure, and I could tell that I was beginning to run a fever.

"I'm so sorry I gave them to you, Sister Charity," Sister Phoebe told me. "I feel responsible."

"It isn't your fault. You didn't know."

Actually, we weren't even supposed to sympathize with each other. That was a sign of giving in to the flesh.

I didn't know what to do. I wanted to take a bath, but I had taken one two days before and didn't think I deserved another.

Sick and miserable, I crawled into my sleeping bag and prayed that God would give me strength and help. I had no words for my prayer. It was a silent crying out to God from the depths of my tortured body. Brother Evangelist had been right in saying that such times taught us to depend upon God. I learned much about praying earnestly during the time I suffered with mites.

That very afternoon, another sister had told me I was having trials because I was accustomed to giving in to the flesh and had to learn to discipline myself.

She had been sitting on her sleeping bag next to me when I crawled into my bag, covered up my head and started crying. I don't know whether she was unsympathetic or didn't know what to do to help me—we had never had a great deal in common—but she acted as though she had not even heard me. Finally I went to the room one of the married brothers and his wife shared. I was weeping uncontrollably.

"Get into your sleeping bag," he told me, "but you'd better get those sores washed first."

I was grateful for his admonition to wash. Had he not told me to, I would not have been able to do so without the risk of deep feelings of guilt. Now I was free to wash as often as I wanted. For as long as we were in the migrant camp, I washed twice a day. Although my sores felt better after washing, I was still plagued by the parasites.

I was not the only one who was infected. A number of other sisters had them, too. Brother Evangelist would call us to the front during our nightly gatherings and have us kneel so the older brothers could lay hands on us and pray for us. Until that moment, I had not considered the inconsistency in making it permissible for them to lay hands on us when it was such a sin to touch us at any other time. I suppose the fact that they were praying made it acceptable.

"Through our suffering we are encouraged," Brother Evangelist said, mentioning Job and his suffering with boils. "This is just a trial the Lord is putting you through."

Sister Phoebe's sores spread rapidly. In the morning they would swell up and be filled with pus. I found her one morning sitting on the sidewalk outside our building, her head in her hands. She hadn't felt able to eat, and was miserable and helpless.

According to the rules Brother Evangelist set down, we were never to approach one of the brothers with a request for someone else. But this was different and Brother Micah was different. I found him and told him about her. He went to her quickly.

Brother Micah talked with her for a few moments and when he left he patted her hand. The act touched me. He had such compassion that I don't think he was actually aware that he had touched her. And she seemed to reach out for his affection.

The migrant camp had only a cold shower and Sister Phoebe was desperately in need of hot water and a tub. I heated some water for her and the brothers allowed her to take a bath.

The exertion of getting into the tub and out again was so exhausting to her that I had to help her back to her sleeping bag. Sister Phoebe's fever was high, and I was concerned. Had I been allowed to do so, I would have gotten someone to take her to a doctor—but I could not. So I sat beside her until she finally fell asleep.

The next day more of my bites were infected, too. I followed her through the entire cycle. Then, for no apparent reason, my bites got worse than hers. One of the brothers suggested that a concoction of Vaseline and alcohol might help. I approached Brother Micah and he gave me permission to try it.

I had been told this would smother the mites and might help the infection. I smeared the stuff all over my body and put on some other clothes underneath my regular garb. I had just finished when another brother came around.

"Sister, it would be good if you would work on the meal today, praise God," he said.

I groaned inwardly. I didn't see how I could do it, but I could not refuse. *Don't complain,* I told myself. I set to work, thinking that I could not keep moving for another minute. I not only helped prepare the meal, I scrubbed floors afterwards—on my hands and knees.

By the end of the day I was hot and sweaty and dirty. I wanted only to drag myself off to bed. But there was another gathering scheduled after the evening meal, and not attending such a meeting was unthinkable.

While the gathering went on, I could only think that I needed to put on more of the greasy concoction. Or change it . . . or *something*. Then remorse swept over me. That wasn't what I needed at all—I needed to trust the Lord. I was supposed to forsake the world and trust God for all my needs. The mental battle continued until long after the gathering ended. Finally I went to the sisters' room and washed it all off. But I was so itchy and uncomfortable, I put it back on. Then, under conviction once more, I washed it off for the second time.

The following morning I went to Brother Evangelist and told him what had happened. He had not been in camp when I was given the Vaseline and alcohol to put on my sores. I explained how I had received victory over my desire to turn to the world to help me out of my discomfort.

"That's right, Sister," he said. "I just encourage you to trust in the Lord. He has healed several cases of mites in this group and He will heal you, too."

After that, I didn't use anything on them. The following day Brother Evangelist came to me and asked if I could go on the road.

"The Lord willing, I can," I answered meekly, trying somehow to generate enthusiasm and confidence that I would be able to travel.

Slowly I gathered my gear and rolled up my sleeping bag. I always sought to do the Lord's will. Everybody else was leaving, so I thought God was guiding me to go, too. The sores on my hands and arms made the preparations difficult, but once more I took to the road.

12
Those Awful Days

This time I was assigned to travel with two of the brothers I had never been with before. It was January, and after leaving the migrant camp we were hitchhiking along a well traveled highway.

Except for the mites, I had enjoyed our stay in Florida and wished we could have lingered there until the sun had coaxed the trees to bud at our destination somewhere to the north. But that was not to be. Brother Evangelist informed us that the Lord had told him He wanted us to take the message of salvation to others, so we were moving out.

The first day on the road was difficult for me and we hadn't traveled far by nightfall. The brothers stopped at a little abandoned railroad house of some kind, situated between the tracks and the highway on the edge of a sleepy little town.

Although neither of the brothers mentioned my affliction, I am sure the infected bites that covered my arms and hands had been responsible for their choosing the little building as a place to sleep. We were still far enough south for warm weather, and ordinarily they would have simply stopped by the side of the road. One of the brothers went inside, looked around and came back to where I was standing.

"Sister," he said gently, "there is a sink up there if you want to wash your sores."

I thanked him and made my way into the building. But the water was cold and did nothing to ease the infection that by this time was spreading over my entire body. The ugly, red ulcerations itched violently and were extremely sensitive to the touch.

I looked down at my soiled garb, remembering how careful Mom had always been about keeping spots of infection clean. If only I had some newly-washed clothes to put on, or even some fresh white underclothes.

Back at the camp where warm water was available I could soak my arms until the scabs would soften and the putrefaction could ooze out. With only cold water, however, I had to scrape off the scabs to get relief. It was a painful operation but finally I finished and was able to crawl, miserably, into my sleeping bag. As I lay there, feeling the fever rise, I thought again of home and how Mom had cared for me when I was ill. I remembered my room with its comfortable bed and clean, crisp sheets. As my fever increased during the night I longed for Mom in a way that I had not longed for her since I joined the group. I could almost feel her soft hands on my forehead.

I tossed restlessly and wished the night away. Toward morning I did manage to sleep a little, but as dawn began to lighten the sky I awakened and dragged myself out of my sleeping bag. I was in such pain I could not stay on the floor any longer. I had to go through the ordeal of taking care of my sores again and getting my gear together. I knew the brothers would be up soon, anxious to be on the move again. Getting around that morning turned out to be more difficult than I had expected, and I had only finished washing myself when there was a gentle knock on the door.

"Sister, we must be on our way."

"I'll be ready in a few minutes." By this time I was in such agony that I took no care to hide my emotions as we were directed to do. I was crying openly. I forced myself back to the room where I had slept and was jolted back to reality by the sight of my sleeping bag. I still had to roll it up, and the holy brothers were waiting. Well, I reasoned, tears streaming down my cheeks, they would just have to wait. I was working as fast as I could.

Clumsily I attempted to make a roll of the sleeping bag, but my left hand was swollen to twice its normal size and I could not bend my wrist or use my fingers. Finally I had to resort to using my elbows. The pain and frustration were more than I could bear. By the time I was finally ready to go I was sobbing. I knew the brothers were able to hear me through the flimsy walls, but I was in such agony that it no longer mattered.

I wanted to ask them to roll up my sleeping bag, but the hold of that cardinal law of the cult was too strong. I could not force myself to ask their help. Looking back, I am sure they were wrestling with the same problem, but like me, they had decided that God could not be blessed by such actions.

When I was finally ready one of the brothers turned to me, concern in his eyes. "The Lord must really be blessing you with this blessed trial, Sister. Praise God."

Before returning to the road we sang a song and they both prayed. I don't remember the name of the song but the lyrics went something like, "We came this far by faith. Don't be discouraged."

My swollen hands made even sitting still uncomfortable, and that was impossible. We were on the move. I don't know how I was able to travel during those awful days.

My left hand was worse than the right. At first I took comfort in that, thinking I was right-handed and the Lord was blessing me by allowing my right hand to be better than my left. It soon became apparent, however, that I was going to have difficulty in using either hand. The pain was so great that I became increasingly concerned about the infection.

The brothers reminded me often that the Lord had singled me out for special blessing. That was the reason for my affliction. "He only sends trials for our own benefit," they repeated again and again.

But their words were empty and meaningless. I felt like telling them that I could do without quite so much blessing, but the instant the thought came I was convicted. My doubts and fears and inner rebellion were attacks of the devil, I reminded myself. I was determined to find out what God was trying to tell me. Perhaps He wanted me to read my Bible more. The more I thought about that, the more convinced I became that I had learned the reason for my trials.

I began to spend every possible moment with my Bible open. It wasn't easy to sit, especially cross-legged. It hurt so much just to remain in one position for more than a few minutes, and every time I moved my rough clothes scraped over the sores and places of infection. No matter how hard I tried, it was impossible for me to concentrate on my reading.

I had heard the brothers mention something about going to Pennsylvania. Mentally I tried to compute the distance and how long it would take to get there. I felt that if we could only reach a place where we could stop and not have to go through the torture of unpacking and packing and hitching rides, I would be better.

But there were miles and miles and miles to go, and more terrible nights of sleeplessness than I thought I could bear. I went through a period of diligent Bible study—as diligent as I could manage in my condition—adding prayer upon prayer that God would be satisfied with my sincerity and remove my torment. Finally I reached the place where I was too listless and miserable even to go through the motions of Bible reading. Whenever I had opportunity to do so I sat, staring out into space with eyes that scarcely comprehended the scene around us.

We were getting far enough north that it became cold and snowy, but we still had a long way to go. In spite of the cold, however, I decided to leave my coat behind. It was almost too small for me and over my heavy, loose-fitting clothes, it pressed painfully against my ulcerated body.

Each day the pain seemed to increase. I could not believe it possible to ache and throb any more than I was, but every day the pain became stronger. I must have been a miserable sight. My arms and hands were swollen and the scabs that almost covered me oozed pus—a dirty, yellow, terrible smelling putrefaction that was offensive to everyone who got close to me.

I couldn't wash while we were traveling, but I knew that I had to get those scabs off. I had seen mites on some of the other kids and when the scabs were left the sores spread and refused to heal. They had to be opened and kept open. Once when I changed into my other set of clothes I used some of those little handy-wipes to scrape the scabs away. When I ran out of them I used my finger nail.

At least two nights during the trip I sat on my pack all night. It was simply too painful to open it up and have to face rolling it up again the following morning. I remember one of those nights particularly. The sun had set and a misty haze had settled over the quiet countryside. I could hear the steady, rhythmic breathing of the brothers from their camping area thirty feet away. The biting cold wind whistled through the shelterbelt they had chosen for our overnight camping place. I was physically exhausted from the travel and the continuous fever.

The darkness spread, and through a tiny break in the clouds I caught a glimpse of the bright moon. Memories flooded over me. This was the same moon that was looking down on Denver and my parents. I wondered if they still thought about me, if they ever looked up as I was doing and wondered if I was watching that same silver ball in the sky. I knew the printing plant kept Dad very busy. Perhaps he was working overtime again. If that were true, he wouldn't have much time for thinking.

Mom and Dad always talked about doing God's will.

Did they accept the things that I told them in my letters? Would they understand? How I prayed they would. I wanted them to know that I still loved them, in spite of the fact that I had been gone so long and hadn't been in touch with them, except for the few times I had written.

One of the brothers turned restlessly in his sleeping bag and I was jarred back to the present. We had been warned by Brother Evangelist that there would be times of trials—times when we would be tempted by thoughts of our flesh people. I was embarrassed to think that I had been so weak as to allow myself to be caught up in thoughts of the world. Yet, Mom and Dad knew what I believed. They wanted all of their kids to go to Heaven. They weren't trying to be a snare. They would be anxious to help me in my Christian life. As I watched and thought, the haze once more covered the moon and the sky was dark again.

I put my head on my arms and told God how miserable I was. "God," I said quietly, "I am so worn out and so tired. I haven't slept for such a long time and every day on the road is too much. I don't know how much longer I can take this. Please, God, somehow send me some relief."

I remained motionless for five or ten minutes, until the glare of headlights penetrated the gloom. In that instant I realized the car was going to stop. I don't know how I knew—I just did.

The vehicle started past us, then braked to a halt not far from where I was sitting. Fear mixed with my relief as I saw the large emblem of the State Highway Patrol come into focus on the car door.

Often the police were not very nice to us and I had no reason to believe this officer would be any different. I stiffened involuntarily as he got out of the car and walked toward me. He stood for a moment several feet away, looking down at me.

"Do you have a place to stay for the night?" he asked. His voice sounded as though it had come from Heaven.

By this time the brothers were standing behind me. "The Lord provides," one of them said, giving the stock answer they were taught to give whenever the police approached.

Hope died within me as the officer continued his questioning. He wanted to know who we were, where we were from and what we were doing.

"We are just serving the Lord," the brother who was speaking for all three of us said, "and the Lord provides."

The officer looked over at me and then at my companions. "The Lord just provided!" he exclaimed. "Get your things together and get into the squad car. It's too cold out here. A dog shouldn't be out on a night like this."

"Where are you taking us?" the spokesman demanded. "To jail?"

"I'm taking you to the Mission for the night. They'll give you a warm bed and a hot cup of coffee."

How I thanked God as I got into the back seat of the warm, dry police cruiser. I had almost forgotten what it was like to be warm again.

The hostess at the Mission met me warmly. I could see the concern on her kind face as she surveyed me, wet and dirty and shivering.

"Would you like to take a hot bath to warm you up before you go to bed?" she asked.

What a blessing it was to soak in a hot tub and clean away the filth from my ulcerated body. "Praise God!" I whispered. And this time I truly meant it. He had answered my prayer out on that highway.

When I was dressed again I went to find the hostess. "I have this infection," I said, rolling up the sleeve of my heavy robe and revealing my arms.

She looked at them and gasped. "My dear child! Why didn't they tell me when you registered that you had this infection? They should have phoned a doctor and gotten a prescription for you."

"It's all right. We just trust the Lord. He will take care

of it." And then I thought of the officer and this gentle, compassionate woman. "God brought me here so I could have a warm bath and get the sores cleaned up."

"I've got some ointment for you," she said. Turning to the dresser to get the antibiotic cream, she told me that she trusted the Lord, too. "My little boy fell and skinned his knee and got a severe infection. I had this cream the doctor had given us for another infection, so I began to use it and pray. His knee healed. We didn't take him to the doctor, but I believe the Lord can use doctors and medicine. Before you go to bed tonight, I want you to put it on your sores."

I tried to explain to her how we lived. The officer had told the man who registered us that I was sitting alone beside the road, cold and dirty and tired, while the brothers slept nearby, not caring about me. I tried to make her understand about that, too.

"They would help me," I said, "but that would be weak, giving in to the flesh. This is a trial that I have to go through. God is trying to teach me something." I went on to tell her that the brothers and the group meant much to me.

"I'm sorry," my new friend said, "but I don't understand how your loving, godly brothers won't do more to help you with this infection. And I still think they should get you to a doctor."

She could not understand, I told myself, but I knew why. I had been taught well by Brother Evangelist and the rest. I was striving, desperately, to be a good soldier for the Lord and not allow the brothers to know how miserable I was. They had no way of knowing about the fever, nor did they know that the pus built up in the sores because I hadn't been able to wash them properly. They didn't even know about the two nights I had sat up, leaning on my pack because I didn't have the strength to unroll my sleeping bag. I hadn't let them know how I sang and prayed and watched the moon move slowly across the sky.

I hadn't dared tell anyone about the night I had thought of going off the freeway and hitching on without the brothers, going anywhere I could to get away from them. Nor had I explained how swiftly remorse had come and how I sobbed silently, begging God to forgive me.

I felt guilty using the antibiotic cream the kindly young woman gave me, but I was sleeping in a bed the Mission was providing, and she had asked me to use the cream. The brothers had taught me to be submissive and polite. I might have offended her if I had refused, so I felt justified in using the cream—even though it was against the teachings of Brother Evangelist.

The soothing warmth of the hot bath soon began to wear off, and the sores began to itch again. I desperately wanted something to give me relief, but even as I rubbed the ointment on I felt as though I was going against everything I had been taught since joining the group. Finally my remorse and bewilderment was overcome by exhaustion and I drifted off to sleep.

We continued on our way the next morning. I didn't tell the brothers that the woman had offered medication and that I had used it. I knew they would not approve. In a gas station where we stopped to use the rest rooms I took off my smock and soaked my sores. Although they had not scabbed during the night because of the medicine, they were beginning to scab again. And even without a thermometer I knew that my fever was coming back.

There was a light rap on the door. "Sister Charity," one of the brothers said, "you must be diligent. The station manager isn't happy with our presence, especially since we aren't purchasing gas." Hurriedly I washed off the sores and put my smock back on. I thought of Job and his suffering. At least I didn't have any dogs come and lick the sores.

That trip was probably the most difficult of any I had ever made. Several mornings we awoke to snow blowing around us and one night we shared a meal at a picnic table when the wind was blowing so savagely we couldn't keep things on the table. The nights were horrible. I will always remember, gratefully, the gas station attendant who allowed us to sleep in the back of one of his U-Haul trucks parked beside the station.

The days overlapped, and it always seemed that I would never manage to live through the next twenty-four hours, but somehow we were able to work our way north until we met the rest of our people in Norristown, Pennsylvania. By the time we got there the infection was beginning to heal. Once I was able to wash daily, the last traces left and I was well again.

The dear sister who had originally given me the mites helped to take care of me and became my closest friend. While she helped me bathe and take care of those ugly sores we talked quietly about the nights in Florida, when we had been unable to sleep because of the itching and discomfort. We remembered how we sat and sang softly and brushed each other's hair, how we rubbed each other's feet in order to be a comfort to each other.

Neither of us mentioned the fact that, like so many who suffer hangovers when they get drunk, or court cancer when they smoke, we also had asked for much of the suffering we endured. We didn't sin in the same way those people did, but our lifestyle brought on many of our problems.

I was bewildered by the way the leaders of our group insisted that we abuse our bodies, which were created and given to us by our Heavenly Father. The gap between what I had learned as a child and what I had been taught by Brother Evangelist was widening. And I was not all that sure which side I really wanted to be on.

Gradually, however, my doubts were brushed aside— at least for a time. I began to get back my strength, and became involved in the daily camp routine.

13
Interlude

The next eight or nine months were relatively quiet. For some reason no one was able to understand, there was a lull in the active pursuit of the group by our flesh people. It was almost as though they had completely given up trying to get us back.

We were warned that was not to be. Brother Evangelist informed us again and again that they would strike when we least expected it, and if we weren't vigilant, some of our beloved brothers and sisters would be snatched from the very portals of Heaven and thrown into the eternal fire.

I don't know why Brother Evangelist kept us moving during this period, but he did. After a month in Pennsylvania we went to Fitchberg, Massachusetts for three months. From there we traveled to Portland, Maine, where we stayed for four long months. After leaving there we hopped about, staying a week in New Paltz, New York and the same length of time in Hartford, Connecticut and Burlington, Vermont.

During that time we were constantly being drilled on the interpretation of the Bible. "We are not going to fall to Satan's wiles," Brother Evangelist thundered. "We are going to study the Word and learn all that God reveals to us. We're going to reinforce our belief in the ways of our group and the Christian faith and strengthen ourselves in regard to our flesh people, so we will be ready when the trouble begins again."

Brother Evangelist seemed able to read the hearts of each of us. Those he felt were not strong enough in the faith had special lessons and Scriptures. He encouraged us to keep notebooks and be diligent in filling them with gems of wisdom from the gatherings. Most of those choice statements came from his lips, but we didn't notice that. All we saw was that the Bible supported him in everything he said. I was to realize much later that this came about because he chose his references carefully—a verse or two here, a sentence there, a phrase from still another portion. They were jerked completely out of context.

Much of what he said paralleled the teaching of my parents, but other portions were disturbing. Like his refusal to accept the Trinity.

In one of the gatherings he began to talk about the oneness of God. "In 325 AD," he began, "some wicked, carnal men who wanted to strike a devastating blow to the plan and purposes of God, came up with the Trinity. It is a lie! Probably the greatest lie man has ever perpetrated."

I gasped audibly and two or three brothers and sisters glanced quickly at me. But I couldn't help it. I had always been taught the Trinity and had believed it completely—as completely as I believed that Jesus Christ is the Son of God. Until that afternoon I had not been aware of the fact that Brother Evangelist did not accept the truth of the Trinity.

He may have mentioned his denial of the Triune God in one of the earlier gatherings I attended. He probably did. But I hadn't realized it. Now, however, there was no denying where he stood on the matter. Where we *all* stood—for we believed what he believed. That was what we had been taught. Brother Evangelist had a clear revelation from Almighty God. God spoke to us through him, so we had to accept it. Our doubts and questions were sin.

But this was most difficult for me to accept. It went so counter to what my parents and our church had taught me. I waited for him to continue.

"It's a lie," he repeated, "because God dwells completely in Jesus Christ. The spirit was not given to Him in measure, like it was to you and me." I did not understand his explanation. I'm not sure anyone did, but we dared not ask about it. That would be akin to blasphemy.

". . . The fullness of God dwelt in Him. Every bit of God dwelt in Jesus. He was the express image or mirror-image of God." Brother Evangelist paused, his piercing eyes searching our faces. "No man could actually see God. He is too great—too glorious—too perfect— so God manifested Himself in flesh and called His name Jesus. Even the devil knows there is just one God, but he is trying his best to trip people up. He is trying to make each of you believe that there are three gods, four gods, a thousand gods. He doesn't care how many gods you believe in, as long as you ignore and deny the only living God. He knows that God is Jesus and trembles. Jesus said this when He was on earth. It is so simple. And yet man has to complicate it. In his carnality he comes up with the doctrine that there is not one God, but three. God the Father, God the Son and God the Holy Spirit! What a dastardly trick of Satan!"

I listened. I can still hear his words beating on my ears, but I did not know what to believe. That night I lay until long after midnight, pondering what he had said. I wrote down his words as closely as I could remember, and the next few days I went back to the Scriptures and tried to understand the verses he said that proved God is Jesus and Jesus is God and there is no Trinity.

It was difficult for me to follow his reasoning. He said there is no Trinity, yet he talked about the Holy Spirit. I suppose the problem lay in his interpretation of the Holy Spirit. Still, he made no attempt to explain.

I hoped he would continue on the subject but,

although he came back to it from time to time, he went on to other things. As the lessons continued I began to sense an intolerance on the part of Brother Evangelist and the elders for children. He introduced the subject with Proverbs 29:15: "The rod and reproof give wisdom: but a child left to himself bringeth his mother to shame."

"The rod has to be used frequently to bring the child under subjection," he taught. "It is not enough to limit your correction to words."

" 'Train up a child in the way he should go: and when he is old, he will not depart from it,' " he quoted. "There is a war going on. We must be strong in the Lord and punish when punishment is due. The flesh of our children is warring against us. As we're caught in a host of activities during the day, there is a temptation for us not to devote ourselves as completely to the Word of the Lord as we should. But children have no work. All they have to do is to war against us."

I shuddered, thinking of my darling nieces and nephews. How could they have been tools of evil?

"But," he continued, "we have to be careful not to justify ungodliness in children. 'Withhold not correction from the child; for if thou beatest him with the rod, he shall not die. Thou shalt beat him with the rod and shalt deliver his soul from hell . . . He that spareth his rod hateth his son: but he that loveth him chasteneth him betimes.' "

It was not the Bible verses Brother Evangelist used that disturbed me, nor even what he said about discipline. I knew that my own father would have agreed with them. It was more a matter of emphasis that upset me, the way his lips curled about the words and his eyes flashed. I had the uneasy feeling that his idea of discipline and chastening with the rod was poles apart from that which Dad subscribed to—discipline tempered with love and compassion and concern.

" 'Foolishness is bound in the heart of a child,' " Brother Evangelist said sternly. " 'But the rod of correction shall drive it far from him.' "

I thought back to the time in Florida when several of the sisters, including myself, had been sleeping in a large room in the same building where a married couple with a year-old baby also had a room. Not long after we had gone to bed the baby started to cry fitfully. It sounded to me like the sort of fussing my nieces and nephews had done when they were teething.

The child's father, however, disregarded the fact that the child might be ill. Twice or three times he ordered her to be quiet. When the child did not stop crying immediately, we heard a resounding slap as he struck her. Immediately she began to wail even louder than before.

"I said stop that!" Again he hit her—harder this time. "I told you to shut up!" Each time he spoke he struck the frantic child.

"What's the matter with that brother?" One of the sisters whispered to me. "Doesn't he realize that she's sick?"

I shook my head.

The baby kept crying and her father kept striking her and ordering her to be quiet, while we sisters lay there suffering in the agony of knowing the little one was being abused and being unable to do anything about it. Finally the girl lying next to me got up.

"I can't stand this!" she exclaimed.

"You aren't going in there, are you, Sister?" I demanded, horrified at the thought.

"No, I'm going outside."

"I'll go with you."

We left the building quietly and walked far enough away so we could not hear the screaming of the baby. We stayed for an hour or more, until the frenzied little one had finally gone to sleep.

The next morning we saw that her little face was bruised, but we dared not say anything about it. Now, I wondered if this was the sort of thing Brother Evangelist was talking about.

The following study was on our attitude toward our parents. We had gone over this many times in the months I had been within the group. I thought I had heard every argument that could be raised for turning away from our flesh people. This time, however, he stressed the Scriptures more than reason. He began by reading John 3:3-6, a portion any evangelical Christian would subscribe to without reservation.

" 'Jesus answered and said unto him, Verily, verily I say unto thee, Except a man be born again, he cannot see the kingdom of God. Nicodemus saith unto him, How can a man be born when he is old? can he enter the second time into his mother's womb, and be born? Jesus answered, Verily, verily, I say unto thee, Except a man be born of water and of the Spirit, he cannot enter into the kingdom of God. That which is born of the flesh is flesh; and that which is born of the Spirit is spirit.'

"The first time we are born," Brother Evangelist told us, "we are born to our flesh parents. The second time we are born, it is to our spiritual parent. Now, God is my Father. He is *your* Father.

"There is usually a period of rebellion with children, during which they revert back to the characteristics and sins of their parents." He paused for a moment. "I need to hate my own life," he continued. "Hate projecting about myself and hate projecting myself to my parents."

If you have difficulty understanding that, you are no more confused than I was. I still am not sure just what he meant by that last sentence.

"To have an image of our own selves is bad," he said. "What we really need to relate ourselves to as children of God is love. The people of the world are suffering from narcissism, where people love themselves."

I thought I was well versed in the Bible, especially since I joined the group, but I was completely bewildered by his arguments.

" 'And call no man your father upon the earth,' " he

read with obvious delight, " 'for one is your Father, which is in Heaven.

" 'For though ye have ten thousand instructors in Christ, yet have ye not many fathers: for in Christ Jesus I have begotten you through the gospel.' "

There were other verses he quoted and explained to us, drawing out the conclusion that we were to turn from our flesh parents, but he saved the clincher for the climax of his lesson.

" 'And there went great multitudes with him: and he turned, and said unto them, If any man come to me, and hate not his father, and mother, and wife, and children, and brethren, and sisters, yea, and his own life also, he cannot be my disciple.'

"There you have the Scriptural proof of the proper attitude toward our flesh parents. We are to hate them. Do you understand that? It's what the Word of God says. That's right! We're to hate our parents! Anything less is unacceptable to God."

Again that night I could not sleep. Ever since I had joined the group I had been taught that my place as an unmarried sister was one of humility and submission. I could not expect to understand the Scriptures the way the brothers understood. And particularly the way Brother Evangelist understood. I had to listen carefully to his messages at our gatherings and make copious notes so I could study the truth. For months I had accepted the fact that the brothers knew more about the Bible than I could ever know.

Now my mind was reeling. I knew Brother Evangelist's interpretation was faulty, yet I had been so programmed that I found it difficult to accept the fact that he was wrong.

14
New York City

From Vermont we made our way to New York City, where Brother Evangelist decided it would be all right for us to live in buildings. Our way of life and our mode of dress made us quite conspicuous and he was concerned about the continued pursuit of our flesh people. There was more security inside, he explained, and our activities would more likely be hidden from the prying eyes of Satan's followers.

I don't remember who located the first building we moved into, but it was in a smelly, broken-down section of the Bowery. Three brothers, another sister and I were assigned to move into it first and begin the long, difficult task of cleaning it up. Undoubtedly it had furnished shelter for an untold number of derelicts and winos who wandered aimlessly up and down the refuse-filled streets in that decaying section of the city. The rooms were so filthy I didn't think we would ever be able to get them cleaned. We literally shoveled out the garbage—great baskets and boxes of it.

But even that was not enough. We needed large quantities of soap or some other strong cleansing agent. Brooms and scrub brushes and cold water were not enough. After the brothers scrounged through the neighborhood and found ammonia cleanser, we spent hours scrubbing the floors and walls with it. Although we were able to do little to materially improve the looks of the interior, it smelled clean and fresh when we finished—far better than it had when we first set to work the week before.

The brothers spent a great deal of time prowling the streets and alleys, looking for things that would be of use to us. They located a couple of refrigerators and an old stove, which they brought to the house and fixed up. One of our group had worked as an electrician, so he was able to bypass the meter box and give us electricity. Another had worked with plumbing long enough to be able to repair the leaking pipes and turn the water on.

The fact that the city didn't know we were there and was furnishing us with power and water without payment did not seem to bother the brothers. In fact, Brother Evangelist had a way of rationalizing such actions.

"It is not wrong for us to take the things we need from the waste of the world," he told us. "Christ did the same when He and His disciples went through the field and picked kernels of corn to eat. It is not wrong for us to do the same. There is such evil within *this* generation of vipers that it is not sin for us to take what we need. We are justified in our acts as children of light dealing with the children of darkness."

Brother Evangelist forbade us to go out on the streets to solicit money or sell candy or pins or flowers in the manner of some groups. If we were offered a donation, which happened occasionally, we took it and brought the money back to the elder brother in charge, but we wouldn't ask for anything.

When the house was cleaned and we had moved in, our leader sent us out to Central Park or one of the many shopping areas to share Christ. We were careful in our witnessing, trying to find the people God would actually have us talk to. I began to look for those who seemed lonely and depressed. New York had to be filled with them, I thought.

We were taught to be selective when we shared our

faith in Christ. The brothers explained that only a chosen few would listen when we approached them. That meant that most of the people on the streets would be unresponsive. How would I select those to speak to and those to avoid? It was not an easy decision.

Some of the sisters I went out with tried to talk to many people and often would get into arguments. When that happened I would think, *You shouldn't have talked to that person. You should have been more selective.* My attitude began to affect my own witnessing until I scarcely talked with anyone.

I heard so many people speaking against what we were doing that I dreaded going out to witness. I felt as though nobody cared. I even mentioned it to one of the sisters—a dear friend I could trust to keep my confidence. "I go out and tell people I have peace," I confessed, "but when I come back here I realize that I don't have peace at all."

"Maybe you need to wait on the Lord," she told me. "Brother Evangelist has always told us that we need to study and learn more, Sister."

I pulled out my notebook and turned to what I had written from the gatherings on witnessing. The verses I had recorded were those we had learned at home and in church and at Nebraska Christian High School. One verse, Proverbs 14:25, was constantly stressed by Brother Evangelist. " 'A true witness delivereth souls.' " I looked it up in my Bible and wondered why our leader had not mentioned this last portion: " '. . . but a deceitful witness speaketh lies.' "

Almost as though in answer to my questions, Brother Evangelist devoted another gathering to the problems encountered in sharing Christ. He taught again the concept that we were either good witnesses or bad witnesses. If we lived a consistent Christian life, others would see it in our lives. As he spoke I decided that this was my problem. I determined to study more than ever before and to be careful of the way I lived so I could bring others to Christ.

As winter approached, my thoughts only occasionally returned to Colorado and the holiday season that was rapidly approaching. When Sister Agatha and I were out witnessing we stole a glance at the date on the newspapers at the vendor's stand. It was December 10, 1976. Even to remember the date was considered a sign of decadence and worldliness. According to our leader it revealed a concern for paganism and the things of this world. To be interested in the date at this time of year, especially, was enough to bring us a severe reprimand, but we were alone and were such close friends that we would not tell anyone else of the indiscretion. Besides, if there was guilt, we were both guilty.

We did not have to see the date, however, to know that Christmas was not far away. The streets were decorated and as we walked there was an air of happiness. The warm greeting of the season, "Merry Christmas," was heard everywhere. I was not merry, however. This was the second Christmas in my life when I wasn't looking forward, expectantly, to that glorious day. I had always loved the season above all others—particularly the music. It was so beautiful I wanted to cry.

As we walked, the words of the brother who had spoken at the morning gathering, ran through my mind. "Christmas is an unholy day," he had said. "Professing Christians have a big part in this. The merchants of the earth have waxed rich through the abundance of merchandise.

"Most of the holidays that are the so-called Christian church observances are not holy days at all. They are merely feast days and have their origin in the excesses of the pagan world.

"Open your Bibles to Jeremiah 10:3,4. 'For the customs of the people are vain: for one cutteth a tree out of the forest, the work of the hands of the workman, with the axe. They deck it with silver and with gold; they fasten it with nails and with hammers, that it move not.' That is where our Christmas trees come from.

"The only mention of anyone's birthday in the Bible is when Herod celebrated his and had John the Baptist beheaded. This would surely indicate that God does not regard birthdays.

"He mentioned the birth of His Son only once and that was His actual physical birth. That proves God does not look on birthdays as being important."

I would not have dared to contradict him, but I couldn't completely agree, either. How I loved the story of Jesus Christ's birth. To me, it was of great importance. It revealed how perfectly God had planned for Christ's coming into the world to save us from sin. I found it exciting to recognize that our Lord had begun His life on earth in the lowly atmosphere of a stable in Bethlehem. I was thrilled by the devotion and love of the shepherds and the wise men as they came to honor this Holy Child.

In our own home, Dad and Mom had always made the giving of gifts of secondary importance, and had talked reverently and lovingly of the birthday of the Saviour. Church services and related activities were a major part of our holiday celebrations. In spite of what the brother had said I could not classify my family and their observance of Christmas as pagan and evil.

I had listened intently as he talked of all the sin surrounding those days, and had to admit that much of what he said was true. The gluttony, the widespread use of liquor, the excesses of the world—all were carried on under the guise of celebrating a holy day. "How foolish they are!" he exclaimed, "that they could believe for a moment that God could not see through their 'worship' for what it is."

In obvious disgust he went on to describe, more vividly than I ever could, the world's mockery of God in their holiday celebrations. All in the name of Christianity.

Standing on a street corner one chilly afternoon a few

days later, the strains of "Joy to the World" filtered through the doors of a little church. I could hear the joyous, high-pitched voices of the children as they sang, and found my heart strangely lifted up by that old, familiar song.

It was ironic, I thought, that they should be singing of joy to the world in the midst of all their evil. And I, one of the few chosen ones of Christ, went out on the streets almost daily, trying to tell others of the joy I had found in the group, and so few listened.

As they finished the first carol and started another, a wave of uneasiness swept over me. I was supposed to be experiencing that joy, yet I was feeling it less and less as time passed. I tried so very hard to tell others of the joy I had found, but I realized that many times I was putting forth as much effort to convince myself as I was those I was talking to.

From long association with them, I knew that the sisters who had at first seemed so holy and serene, were as human under the surface as the people in the outside world. There was envy, jealousy, anger, frustration and loneliness in our select little group.

Are we actually any better than the people in the world? I asked myself honestly. I would have given lip service to the fact that we were at peace with ourselves, as children of the Saviour, but deep in my heart I wondered.

I broke the laws and intents of the brothers in other, more subtle ways, although not by design. We were warned repeatedly against forming any close relationships with other sisters. The brothers moved us around frequently, in an attempt to keep us from being tempted to become overly friendly with each other. But that didn't keep us from forming friendships.

It was a joy to me to go witnessing with Sister Agatha. Brother Evangelist would have disapproved of our behavior on some of those trips. We enjoyed each other so much that we often indulged in what he would have termed the sinful worldly wiles of vain talking and foolish babbling.

On this particular occasion, just before Christmas, a light snow was falling as we walked up and down the street. The stores were jammed and the sidewalks were crowded, since it was a night when the merchants were staying open in their quest for worldly gain. Hardly a time for those of us who followed the true way and abhorred such things to be enjoying ourselves. Yet I saw an obvious glow in my companion's eyes as we neared the downtown area. The tree in the window of the corner department store was breathtaking. At the very top was an angel, and a ceramic nativity scene was artfully arranged on a red velvet cloth beneath the tree.

I don't know how long we stood there. Sister Agatha slipped her hand into mine as we stared into the wonderland of Christmases past, when we were at home with our flesh people. The haunting melody of church bells brought us back to reality. We turned to face each other.

"Sister Charity," my companion whispered quietly, "Christmas is an unholy day. It is of the world. Thank God we are out of that."

"Yes," I answered, "praise the Lord." Wistfully, I glanced back at the store window as we turned to walk away. "Praise God we are no longer in that."

We had little to say to each other as we returned to the place where we were living. I was disturbed by the conflicting emotions that churned within me. The brothers were so sincere and they quoted Scripture after Scripture as they explained the true meaning of the Word. I was only a lowly sister. How could I doubt what they were saying?

I had to be more diligent in my studies and Bible reading, I decided. These doubts and fears had to be of Satan—*didn't they?*

15
The Raid

We left New York City some time after Christmas and made our way to St. Louis, where we settled into an old house in an aging section of the city.

Although the brothers did not relax their vigil, frequent witness trips and Brother Evangelist's careful observations indicated that there were no anticipated problems with any of our flesh people. It almost seemed as though they had given up looking for us, or at least had lost track. In spite of that, however, we were careful to cover the windows with blankets and not do anything that would attract attention to ourselves or to the group.

In some of the places where we stayed we were the uninvited guests of landlords who didn't know they were entertaining us. But in St. Louis, the owner of the building lived next door in a house almost as run-down as the one he permitted us to stay in. The brothers went to see him, and made arrangements for us to live in the building free of charge in return for our fixing up the place. The building had been condemned, and he apparently was hoping we would help put it in shape to pass inspection.

Mr. Johnson seemed sympathetic to our religious convictions. At least he didn't criticize. We were even allowed to do our laundry in his apartment building next door. I enjoyed washing in the conventional machine in their basement. It had been so long since I had used a machine and hot water that I had almost forgotten what it was like. It hadn't been easy to get our heavy garb clean by hand, in cold water, with a minimum of detergent. Now the clothes smelled fresh and clean. The coarse fabric was almost soft.

As I carried the laundry back to our apartment building I nestled my face in the stack of clean shirts, feeling something like one of the women on a TV commercial for detergents. That cleanliness! I had not realized how much I had missed it.

When the washing was done and the clothes were put away I took out my sewing. I was making a pack for Brother Zacchaeus. At that moment I felt good about what I was doing and the way we were living. I didn't even mind the separation from my flesh family. We had a place to sleep and food to eat. What more did a child of God need?

I had just begun to work on the pack when Brother Zacchaeus appeared in the doorway of the sisters' room with thread for me to use.

"Praise the Lord," I responded automatically. But inwardly, I was thinking of that morning, when the principle of "do not touch a brother" was again brought to my attention. In the world I had dated a great deal and the men who took me out had not found it so terrible to touch me. It was demeaning to have the brothers go to such extremes to keep from coming into contact with us. Moreover, it was unnatural.

That morning, when Brother Zacchaeus had brought me the material for the pack, he also brought me some straight pins. He handed me the material and I dutifully held out my hand for him to drop the pins into it. In the process his fingers lightly brushed mine. I remembered thinking, *Well, Brother, that wasn't so awful, was it?*

I was shocked by my sudden resentment. I had been with the group for more than a year and a half, and there were times when I felt farther from living up to the standards of the group than when I joined.

I had no way of knowing that before that blustery March weekend was over my life would again be thrown into turmoil. Later I was to learn that my sister and her husband, Sharyn and Jerry Regier, had been attending a conference in Philadelphia at that time. They shared my story with their friends, and all of them prayed together for me.

If the next account sounds sketchy and incoherent in places, there is good reason. Everything happened so fast and there was so much confusion that no one has a concise, accurate picture of exactly what happened.

Jerry Regier was involved in much of what went on. I have chosen to let him tell of the phone call from my parents, of going to St. Louis and enlisting the help of friends there, and of entering the old house to get me away from the group. The following is the way he remembers it.

JERRY REGIER

At the time of our conference in Pennsylvania the Lord laid Rachel heavily on our hearts. It was difficult for us to understand why until a few days later. She had been with the cult for nineteen months and we had heard nothing about her for so long that we had begun to wonder if she was still alive.

At the conference, however, people asked about her wherever we went. We had prayer for her and one of the men who spoke that day chose as his topic, "The Authority We Have in Prayer." Both Sharyn and I found it a great encouragement and we prayed for Rachel with renewed confidence and hope.

The meetings ended on Friday, and around noon the next day her parents phoned to tell us that another member of the cult was out. "She's in Denver," Dad Martin told me. "And they're working with her now. When she comes out of it, we're going to try to talk with her and find out if Rachel has been with her."

I was somewhat reluctant to tell Sharyn about the possibility. Twice before I had gone out on tips, hoping to find her youngest sister, and both times had come home exhausted and empty-handed. I hardly dared hope that this time would be any different. We had a long session of prayer for Rachel and that evening Mr. Martin phoned, again. He had talked to the girl and learned that she had come to Denver from St. Louis to get her husband to join the group. Her husband had managed to spirit her away from her companions and get her deprogrammed. She said that Rachel had been with her in St. Louis.

Dad and I talked for a long while on the phone and finally decided that I would contact a friend in St. Louis and ask him to check it out. In a way, I was reluctant even to go that far. I didn't know if any of us could take the disappointment of looking for her and not finding her again.

As soon as Dad and Mom Martin hung up I phoned my friend in St. Louis. The more we talked, however, the more certain I became that Sharyn's parents wanted me to go down and try to find her. They didn't ask me to go because they had seen the strain the other two futile trips had put on me. They had said that Rachel's uncle from Omaha was going, but I could tell they remembered the previous experiences I had had with the group in Norristown and Amherst and thought it would help if I were in St. Louis, too.

I flew out of Washington early that Sunday morning and got to St. Louis shortly before nine o'clock. One of my friends met me at the airport. In the meantime Mom Martin's brother, Eugene Wyman Sr., and another relative by marriage had been joined by a private investigator and were already cruising around, trying to find the place where Rachel was living. We had all been given the house address that was furnished the Martins by the deprogrammed cult member in Denver.

We met in the area of the house address. I joined Wyman and the others in a car they had borrowed and my friends went on to church. I soon learned that a problem had developed.

"We can't find the house," Wyman announced. A tone of concern edged his voice. "We've looked everywhere, but there isn't a house by any such number."

There was a possibility that the girl had deliberately furnished the wrong house number. If that were true, it was likely that she had lied about other things as well. Rachel might not even be in St. Louis, or the group may have fled. But the girl might have been one number off, or the numbers of the house could have been transposed.

We tried every combination of the numbers we could think of but came up empty-handed. It began to look as though we were defeated again. Yet, since we had come so far, we had to explore every possibility. We were cruising around the general area looking at the houses when I suddenly noticed an old, run-down building with some of the windows blacked out.

I had a strange feeling that our search was over in spite of the fact that the address was nothing like the one we had been given. "I'm sure that's it," I said aloud.

We glanced at each other. There was no doubt that this was the sort of house the cult would be living in, if they were staying in a building. "Now what do we do?" we said to each other.

The detective suggested that we check it out first. That sounded like a good idea. We couldn't go charging into the house without being sure. That would be the best way I knew to bring the police on us—or worse. We were in a predominately black area and could easily be mistaken for narcotics agents, creating a situation that could cause us more trouble than we anticipated—or needed.

So we drove a few blocks up the street, circled the block and came back to a place where we could get a good view of the house without being seen ourselves. We waited tensely, but not for long. In a few minutes a robed man came out of the building and made his way up the street.

"You were right!" Rachel's cousin, Terry, exclaimed. "It *is* the house!"

Now that we had located them we considered storming the place. But there were still sources of potential trouble. We didn't know how many were living there, for one thing. More important, we didn't know for certain if Rachel was with them. While we tried to decide what to do, Terry got out of the car. "I can't stand this sitting," he said. "I'm going to walk around for awhile."

I wasn't sure that was wise but I could understand his growing uneasiness. I think we all felt ready to explode.

"Got your walkie-talkie?" I asked.

He nodded.

"Be careful."

A moment later he was gone, sauntering casually around the back of the house. He found a place behind one of the garbage cans where he could be quite inconspicuous and sat down.

He hadn't been out of the car long when I decided to cross the street to a nearby apartment building. It was aging and almost as decrepit as the house with the blackened windows, but it was occupied. A faded *Apartment for Rent* sign hung on the front doorpost. The glass in the the small, cluttered foyer was broken out. I would be partially concealed if I stood inside and looked out the broken window.

I took my walkie-talkie and tried to use it, but people were going in and out of the apartment house and I was sure they would misunderstand our purpose. So I put it away. A few minutes later Terry joined me, trembling with excitement.

"A girl just came out of the back door with a load of clothes," he whispered, "and went into the apartment house next door. I'm sure it was Rachel!"

I nodded, but I must confess that I didn't really believe him. It could be that I was subconsciously readying myself for another disappointment.

Yet, Terry had married Rachel's cousin and Rachel had sung at their wedding, so he should have known what she looked like. And he seemed so sure that he began to persuade the rest of us he had seen her.

We had done a great deal of thinking and planning about what we would do when we found her—how we would go about getting her away from her fellow cult members. But now that we were faced with the situation we didn't know what we should do. All our well-thought-out plans went down the tubes.

About eleven that morning I phoned the church where my friend attended. I knew we were going to have to go into the house and I was afraid we didn't have enough people. We didn't know how many brothers were in the house, nor how they would react to our intrusion. They considered themselves non-violent, but we weren't exactly sure what they meant by that.

Dave Grey, the fellow who answered the phone, said he had not been able to find my friend John. But he said John had shared Rachel's story with their Sunday school class that morning and they had had prayer for her, and for us.

". . . I sure wouldn't know what to do, Jerry," Dave said, "but if there is any way I can help, I'm available."

I thanked him and asked him to come. "We're going to need all the help we can get."

Dave finally located John and the two of them left church and picked up another Christian friend before coming out to join us. When we were finally assembled, just around the corner from the house, it was almost twelve o'clock noon. We had a brief moment of prayer beside the car, then I assigned people to different locations. I asked Dave and his friend to take up positions in front of the house.

"We've got to cover every exit," I said, "in case they start to run with Rachel." I don't know where I got this mental picture of us going in the back door and frightening the brothers so much they would run out the front door.

I asked Terry to go in with me. Two others went with us inside the big chain-link fence around the back yard. It was a sturdy fence at least twelve feet high, designed to keep prowlers away.

The other two I asked to stay outside and watch the rear of the house while we went inside.

We entered the dilapidated building. In the first room we found three women sitting on the floor.

"We understand you're occupying this house without an occupancy permit," I said, "and that you are here illegally. We would like to see some identification."

They didn't know who we were. "My husband has our identification," one of the women said, "and he's in the house next door."

We didn't realize, then, that the owners of the building actually lived next door and that the woman's husband was visiting them. I would never have gone into the house as we did if I had known the landlord was there and that we were actually trespassing on private property. Being a Sunday, the landlord and his wife were at home.

"I'm going to look through the rest of the house," Terry said.

"What shall *I* do?" I asked him. A fine leader I was. I was supposed to be heading up our determined little band and I was asking advice from my companion.

"Don't let them go!" he called over his shoulder.

That was the best advice he could have given, but I was so rattled I didn't pay attention to it. When the sister offered to go get her husband I allowed her to leave. That was the first big mistake I made.

An instant later Terry came back down the hall. He had Rachel by the hand.

RACHEL
I didn't know anything was going on until someone

opened the door to the room where I was sitting. I looked up from my sewing.

"Rachel!"

I hadn't expected to be called Rachel and it startled me. I was known as Sister Charity by the members of our group.

"You are Rachel, aren't you?"

Although Terry was my cousin's husband I didn't recognize him immediately. I had only met him the one time at their wedding. He walked across the room and took me by the arm. All I could think of was that I was being taken by the deprogrammers—those wicked people I had been hearing about during the past months. Frantically I tried to recall the instructions the brothers had given me.

"Just wait it out," they had said. "Don't speak to them." That, I determined to do. As we came down the hall I saw a familiar figure. I gasped audibly—I couldn't help it. There was Sharyn's husband, Jerry Regier! *Oh, no!* I exclaimed inwardly. *My flesh people have come to take me back into the world!* My heart pounded and my knees went weak. It was all I could do to keep from falling.

JERRY

I stared at Terry and the girl with him in disbelief. I recognized her immediately, although she looked desperately tired and haggard and dirty. She had gained weight and was wearing a coarse, heavy cult skirt and smock. Her arms and face were puffy and her complexion sallow. The Rachel I had known was trim and neat—a vibrant, happy individual with dancing eyes and a quick smile. The girl with Terry was none of those things. Yet I knew it was Rachel. It had to be.

"Praise the Lord!" I said thankfully, as I went over and took hold of her arm.

At that instant three men appeared suddenly in the kitchen and it seemed to me that there were people all over the place. Quickly the brothers sized up the situation.

"Let go of her!"

By this time two of the girls took hold of Rachel's other arm. "You can't take her!"

"But I have permission from her parents," I protested. That was a silly thing to say, since she was of age.

"This is Jerry, my brother-in-law," Rachel told them quietly. Her voice was dull and listless, as though all the strength was suddenly gone from her body and she found it an effort even to talk.

Terry and I froze momentarily. There were so many in the room, all talking at once, and we didn't know what to do. I realized, however, that if we were going to succeed we had to get her out of the house immediately.

We started for the back door. I tried to propel Rachel along and the brothers and sisters tried to jerk my hands away and get her free.

A breathless silence settled over the entire group. There was a struggle. Two of the brothers had wedged themselves in the back door opening so we couldn't get out. One had stuck his head through the screen door and was holding onto the porch railing outside. At the same time he had his feet inside. The brothers were silent and resourceful, doing everything they could to block us but without saying anything.

A couple of the guys with me managed to get the two brothers out of the back door. I don't know how they managed. In fact, I don't even know where they came from unless they followed the brothers inside. But they were able to clear the back door opening. We finally got the door open and forced our way outside. The brothers had moved from the doorway to the back porch, holding onto the steel railings on either side of the steps in a desperate attempt to stop us there. One of our men kicked one of the brothers out of the way and I was able to get Rachel down the five steps, into the back yard, and to the heavy chain-link fence.

The gate was closed and padlocked.

I stopped and glanced around, frantically. I knew the brothers thought they had cut off our only way of escape, and I reasoned that they probably had phoned the police. In many places they had made friends with the authorities.

I looked up at the fence that towered above us and at the barbed wire along the top. There was no way I could scale it, even alone. And with Rachel there was nothing I could do. At this point I'm sure she was incapable of thinking. She was torn between her life with the cult and going with me. She knew how much I loved her, but she was caught up in the twisted thinking of her friends and companions. She walked beside me meekly, as if in a daze.

"Oh, Lord," I prayed helplessly, "what are we going to do? You haven't brought us this far to have us lose her now!"

At that moment two of our men rushed over to the place where the fence joined the building, grabbed hold of the bottom of it, and literally jerked it free. There might have been a little slack in the fence where it was fastened to the post, but I'm sure God gave them special strength. The fence was heavy, comparatively new and well installed. Yet they ripped it free and were able to pull it away from the wall far enough to allow us to stoop over and walk under it. All I could think of was Moses and the Children of Israel when the Red Sea parted and they were able to walk through it to freedom.

As we walked toward the street I suddenly realized that in all of our planning we had made no provision for escape once we had Rachel. All our efforts had been directed toward getting to her, as though that was all that mattered. "Get the car!" I yelled as we crossed the street and started to cross the vacant lot. "Get the car! Get the car!"

By this time the landlord had joined the brothers and they were all converging on the vacant lot, determined to cut off our escape. Now they were yelling again. "She's being kidnapped! She's being kidnapped!" We could hear them as we hurried across the open field.

The landlord caught up with us first. "I'm making a citizen's arrest!" he cried. "I'm making a citizen's arrest!" We looked blankly at him and kept walking.

When we were in the middle of the vacant lot we realized we had a long way yet to go and that they might catch up with us and stop us. We began to run toward the car. One of the brothers called out, "Sit, Sister! Sit!"

Immediately Rachel dropped to the ground.

We dragged her a few feet, but her inert body made it almost impossible for us to move with her. "Somebody get her feet!" I yelled.

I still don't know who responded, but two of our number grabbed her feet and we carried her for the fifteen or twenty yards to the car. When the brothers saw the car they raced to reach it before we did. Our driver spun away from them and turned around on a concrete slab in someone's back yard. As he came roaring up the alley, approaching us for the second time, we were ready. We shoved Rachel into the back seat and I jumped in beside her.

One of the brothers was trying to get in the front door. "Hit it!" I cried. "Hit it!" We took off leaving five of our other guys there.

Seconds later the police pulled up from the other direction. They could have caught us easily, but they didn't know we had gotten away. Our guys split and ran, taking off in all directions. A brother followed each of them. Two of our guys ran off together, running twelve or fifteen blocks with a brother on their tail.

They didn't know where Don and I were taking Rachel and we had not decided on a rendezvous point. Finally, they hailed a cab. As they started to get in, the brother following them approached the driver. "These men kidnapped somebody!" he said.

Our men ignored him and got into the cab. The driver must have been both disturbed and puzzled but he didn't know what was going on and our guys saw no reason to explain. The cab moved half a block before being stopped at a red light. Again the brother came running up and shouted the same thing.

One of our men turned to the driver. "You sure have some weird people in this town."

Rachel's cousin Terry ran through someone's back yard and jumped over a doghouse with a brother right behind him. He kept on going, but he had startled the dog. This big Doberman pinscher came charging out of the doghouse just as the brother came up. Terry's pursuer took one look and retreated, letting Terry get away.

Dave Grey and Gene Wyman were arrested and booked for kidnapping, destruction of property and disturbing the peace. The property damage, they were told, was to the fence.

As we sped away, seeking a safe, quiet place in which to deprogram Rachel, we had little idea of the chaos and turmoil we had left behind. I glanced at my young sister-in-law. After nineteen long months, we had her! I was going to be able to call her parents and tell them their daughter was free. She was out of the cult and they could come and get her.

But, the ordeal was not over yet. As we drove through the streets of St. Louis I didn't know what to say to her. I didn't know how to begin to deprogram her. I knew it was going to be difficult and would probably take a long while, but how were we supposed to go about it? The task seemed so hopeless.

16
God Deprogrammed Me

RACHEL

As we drove away from the area where I had been living, I glanced at Jerry. The lines were deep in his kindly face and I saw the weariness in his eyes. He must have been as concerned about me as my folks and Sharyn, I reasoned.

I don't know why, but I thought then about my note-book and all the questions I had jotted down during the gatherings and my times of personal Bible study. My notebook was back at the house. I might never see it again, but I could recall most of the things I had wondered about. They were permanently etched in my mind and heart.

Jerry should know the answers to all of my questions. He had been through Bible school and was doing Christian work on college and university campuses. And he was the sort who would give me a straight answer, whether it happened to suit his particular purpose or not.

But should I ask him? Brother Evangelist had drilled us well on what we should do if the deprogrammers got us. We had been taught to remain quiet and to refuse to get trapped into conversation with them. Then we were to try to get back to the group as quickly as possible.

I thought about a conversation I had had with Sister Mary a few nights before. We were reading Isaiah 40:31: "But they that wait upon the Lord shall renew their strength; they shall mount up with wings as eagles; they shall run, and not be weary; and they shall walk and not faint."

"Sister Charity," my companion had said, "if your flesh people get you, remember this, God will deliver you! Pray in Jesus' name and if the Lord wants you to get away, He will help you to fly away!"

So I prayed as Jerry and the others got me. I prayed in desperation, "Oh, Lord Jesus, help me to fly away from my enemies!" But nothing happened. At the same time I heard one of those with Jerry praying quietly, "In Jesus' name, help us to get her out of here."

Then I began to realize that I was with Jerry in spite of everything the group had done to get me away from him. That must mean that God wanted me to be with him now.

The overpowering need for answers caused me to forget all my conditioning of the last nineteen months. Again I looked at Jerry. The members of our group had talked a great deal about love, but there was little evidence of it. It was good to be with someone I knew loved me.

"Why are you wearing that ring?" I asked him quietly. "It is ungodly. You shouldn't be wearing it."

He did not reply to my question. "Rachel," he said, "we love you."

Automatically, I protested. "If you loved me, you wouldn't be doing this."

JERRY

We found a motel and I went into the office. I had thought I could get a room and pay for it later. However, they insisted on being paid in advance. I had already decided to use a fictitious name, which meant that I could not use my credit cards. And I had left home so hurriedly I hadn't had time to get any cash. I went out to the car but none of us had enough money to pay the $53 the clerk wanted.

We looked at a few other motels before finding one we thought would be suitable. By this time I had decided to register in my own name and use my credit card, in spite of the fact that it could easily lead the police to us if they checked the motel.

Once we were in the room I looked at my watch. We had gone into the house at twelve noon and were out of the neighborhood in half an hour. Now it was two o'clock and we were just getting a place to stay. Of course, we had taken the time to change cars twice in case anyone was trying to follow us. In spite of that it seemed that much had happened in an incredibly short span of time.

Our concern was not to deceive the police or break the law. We were disturbed only because we were afraid the authorities might take Rachel from us and give her over to the group again. Once we had her deprogrammed and out of the clutches of the cult, we would get the legal implications taken care of. Now our chief concern was Rachel.

I tried to phone Mom and Dad Martin but there was no answer. I didn't know that one of the others had slipped to a booth and called to tell them we had Rachel. They not only were on their way, they were bringing Janet— who had been deprogrammed and told them of Rachel's location—and Nikki Barker with them. Nikki was about the same age as Rachel and had been in the same cult, but had gotten out and had been living with the Martins for the past few months. When they finally caught up with us, she would help with the deprogramming.

But at the moment I was alone, as far as starting to deprogram Rachel was concerned. If I had come up with any practical plan for jarring her to her senses, I had completely forgotten it, now that I was actually faced with the problem.

Fortunately, the Lord took it out of my hands. Rachel began to ask questions. We answered her as directly and as completely as we knew how, right from the Scriptures. Her questions struck at the heart of the cult's doctrines.

She wanted to know about the place of women in God's scheme of things and asked about beauty and vanity. I tried to answer her on that score, but decided it would be better to get a Christian woman to talk with her. When I mentioned that to John, he immediately suggested Dave's wife.

Michelle agreed to come but had some news for us. Her husband and Rachel's uncle, Eugene Wyman, were both in jail. "Our assistant pastor is here for dinner," she said. "You should have seen his face when I told him that my husband couldn't be here because he's in jail."

RACHEL

While we were waiting for Dave's wife to come to the motel I picked up a Gideon Bible that was lying on the desk. I was trying to think of a way to get word to the brothers as to where I was and what had happened. I took a piece of stationery that was lying next to the Bible and was going to write when Jerry and his friend weren't watching. I thought I could put it under the couch with the name of the landlord on it and hope the motel maid would find the note and phone him. But I couldn't remember his name. That must have been of God, because his name, Johnson, could not have been more simple or easy to recall.

Frustrated, I held the Bible in trembling hands, trying to find places to read that would strengthen me for the ordeal I was sure would come. Suddenly I was consumed by a desire to resist Jerry and the others as tools of Satan.

John came into the room and saw that I had the Bible open. "What are you reading?"

I was disturbed by his question. As sisters we were not supposed to quote Scriptures. That was the responsibility of the men. They were to preach and teach.

He sat on the couch beside me. "I've been reading in John 14 lately in my devotions," he said. "It has really been a blessing to me. Would you like to hear it?"

I didn't answer.

"Why don't we read it together?"

Like a proper cult girl I responded. "Whatever you feel led to do," I said.

"If you don't want to, you don't have to," he replied.

"I'm not really led to read the passage right now," I said, tartly, "but if you feel led to read it, I don't mind."

"If you don't want to, we don't have to," he repeated.

I didn't answer, so he began to read. I turned to the same portion to see for sure what it said and when he began to talk about it I found myself listening intently. I thought perhaps I could catch him in something he was wrong on. But, deep inside, there was also a real longing to hear what these men of God had to tell me. I had listened to the brothers for so long. Now I wanted to hear the Word from someone else.

I tried to put on such a front that I found myself being very rude. I was convicted of this, but I said such things to him, I decided, because I didn't want to be nice to the devil. Then I would look at Jerry and the others and realize I was not acting as a believer should. "I'm sorry," I said. "That wasn't very Christian of me."

It wasn't long until Dave's wife came and she and I talked for an hour or more. Jerry and John stayed for a time, but finally decided to leave us alone. When they were gone, Michelle Grey sat on the floor beside me and put one hand on my knee. "You don't have to be afraid of me," she said. "I just want to talk to you."

I didn't look at her.

"You can look at me, Rachel. There is nothing wrong with that. The Lord has given you a pretty face. It isn't a sin to show God's handiwork."

Then I noticed that she was wearing slacks. "Why are you wearing those ungodly pants?" I demanded. "Those are for men. Aren't you supposed to be a Christian?"

"I wear slacks because I am comfortable in them. What I wear isn't important, although I try to be selective and modest in my choice of clothing. It is what's on the inside that counts."

I found myself agreeing with that. After a few moments she sat on the couch beside me and began to play with my hair. "You have beautiful hair," she said. "God gave you such pretty hair and a pretty smile. God gave you the beauty you have."

I argued with her, testily, just as I had argued with Jerry, but I didn't really mean it. I didn't want to go back with the group. There was so much fear among the brothers and sisters and, even though they talked about peace, I had been constantly under pressure. It was good to be back with someone I could trust completely.

I looked around the room. There were some inexpensive pictures on the walls. "Look at those," I said. "That is just vanity in the eyes of the Lord. We need to be working on our spiritual lives. Why do people paint things like that when they should be using their time working for God?"

"That isn't a very good specimen of art, is it?" she admitted softly.

Then she said something that startled me. Both she and her husband had been part of a group for awhile. They had gotten out about five years before. "I know what you are going through," Michelle said.

When Jerry came back into the room a few minutes later I was asking about some more Bible verses that would explain God's place for women—particularly Christian women. She had taken the Bible and found verses that we read together. "Why do you wear a wedding ring?" I wanted to know.

I wasn't prepared for her answer. "I believe that the Lord has given me this man to spend the rest of my life with," she said, quietly. "I want other people to know about this wonderful relationship we have. The love we have is from God and is a part of the love of God. The ring symbolizes to us that there is no beginning and no end to God's love."

I could see how calm and sweet, how meek and quiet

she was. I actually began to think she possessed all the qualities that were so much admired in the group—all the things that we tried so hard to achieve. It came to me that she had what I had been looking for, the very things I had been telling people I had, but did not really possess. Love radiated through everything Michelle said.

As we talked I tried hard to get Jerry and the others to see their sin and disbelief. I told them what the Bible said about hating one's parents, about not becoming attached to the flesh and living for God and becoming part of His family. I also reminded them that they didn't understand what the Word had to say about sobriety, either. I quoted the verses that said we are to be sober, and went on to explain that we were not to laugh.

I can't remember everything Jerry said in refuting my arguments. In fact, I can only remember a little of what he told me. It wasn't his devastating logic that persuaded me. It was his sincerity and his genuine Christian love. That was something the group talked about but showed little evidence of. At around six-thirty that evening, Jerry asked me if I remembered Nikki.

"Of course I do," I said. I remembered the night the two of us had engaged in a great deal of foolishness. We got to laughing over an old-fashioned pair of shoes the Lord had provided for me through the brothers. Our chuckles and giggling got so loud that one of the sisters heard us. The next morning we had been called in by Brother Evangelist and were severely reprimanded for our frivolity.

When Nikki disappeared from the group we thought she had gone back to the world and sin and didn't care about the Lord any more. We supposed that she had taken on seven spirits worse than the one she had before she met the group.

"Did you know that she's on her way here now with your folks?" Jerry asked. "She's been living with them since she got out of the cult."

I smiled. For the first time in nineteen months I

smiled unashamedly and without guilt. It was unbeliev-
able. Here I was with my brother-in-law, and my parents
were on their way to see me.

"I heard you wrote a song, Rachel. Janet shared it
with us."

"Janet?" I looked up incredulously. "You've talked to
her?" The last I had heard, Janet had left St. Louis to go
back to the Denver area to witness to her husband.
Hopefully, she would bring him back to the cult with her.

"Your folks talked with her a couple of days ago,"
Jerry went on. "She's supposed to be with them, too."

JERRY

Rachel's attractive face brightened and a wisp of a
smile appeared on her lips. Slowly it spread to a happy,
excited grin. That was the first time I had seen her smile
since we got her away from the cult.

I had never seen anything quite like it. We can easily
mark the exact moment when the group lost its hold on
Rachel and she came out of her mental bondage. She
started responding and smiling, and acted for the first
time as though she was glad we were there.

Those early hours after her liberation she had been
somber, listening to what we said, but only responding
when she had a question or wanted to challenge us. Now
she sat, reading her Bible. I had never helped deprogram
anyone before and didn't even know what had made the
difference in her. But now I *knew,* and so did the others,
that she was out of it.

Almost at the same time I reached that decision I
heard a car drive up. I was sure of who it was. I could go
out and tell Ken and Lillian Martin that their daughter
was already starting to be herself again.

LILLIAN

Our hearts pounded wildly as we stood outside the
motel that chilly March night, talking with Jerry. For
the first time in nineteen months we would be seeing our

youngest daughter. It still seemed a dream, a wild, joyous dream that we were afraid would soon come to an end. But it didn't. Rachel was there! Just inside the door! And, as Jerry said, she was already free. Whatever hold the cult had on her was broken, and she was eager to be restored to us and return to Denver as our daughter.

We didn't know what to expect in regard to her appearance. When we opened the door she stood for a moment, looking at us uncertainly, as though wondering if we would accept her. But I'm sure she knew!

Without speaking, Rachel ran forward and hugged us both. She was still wearing her cult garb, but she wasn't sitting with her head down and her hair over her face, as we had envisioned. She was much heavier than when we had last seen her in August of 1975, but she was still our attractive, loving daughter.

Our hearts overflowed with praise and thankfulness that God had brought her back to us. He had answered all our prayers and those of our family and friends and concerned believers who had heard about her.

We were even thankful that God had allowed a long span of time to pass before she was restored to us. If she had come back in six months we would have taken for granted the fact that the Lord answers prayer and would have gone on with our lives the same as before. But, as months stretched into a year and finally to nineteen months, we began to realize more completely the blessings of God in giving her back to us.

The night that we had dreamed of for so many long months had finally come. We were a complete family again. Fervently we thanked God for His faithfulness.

RACHEL

One suite of the motel had two double beds. Mom, Janet, Nikki and I shared that room. We pushed the beds together and the four of us slept there.

Janet and I were the first up in the morning. I glanced in the wastebasket beside the desk. There was a

McDonald's sack with a hamburger in it, and Janet and I dug it out and shared it. Mom and Nikki woke up as we were half through. Nikki understood immediately, of course, but Mom was disturbed by it. Janet and I could not understand why, for we were used to eating like that. In fact, the stale hamburger was better than many of the meals we had when we were with the group.

JERRY

Although we had Rachel out of the cult and she was deprogrammed, we still had a serious problem to face. We contacted a St. Louis attorney to help get Rachel's uncle, Gene Wyman, and Dave Grey out of jail. They had both been charged with kidnapping. Dave, however, was released after they questioned him. The police were convinced that he didn't know what was going on.

The charges had been filed by the apartment house owner, including one for destruction of property. The police were out looking for the rest of our "gang." Our attorney had us bring Rachel to the police station, where she signed a deposition stating that she had not been taken forcibly and she didn't want to go back. That would be enough to get the kidnapping charge dropped.

When we arrived at the courtroom we were separated from Rachel, and she was questioned alone. The officers were kindly and talked with her for an hour, making sure she was doing what she wanted to and not what we wanted her to do.

The owners of the building were there and we learned that the charges had grown. We were now charged with malicious destruction of property, trespassing, and disturbing the peace. Janet knew the landlady, having been in the cult recently, and asked the officer in charge if she and Rachel could go over and talk to her. He gave them permission on the promise that they would not try to cause trouble. I went with the girls to talk to her.

The woman was fiercely angry at first.

"You don't realize what we have been in," Janet told

her. "You don't know how many times we wanted to talk to you but weren't allowed to. We were held as though we were in prison."

"I've talked with you girls plenty of times," she countered. "You could come up to my place any time you wanted to."

Incredulously, both Rachel and Janet answered at the same time. "You thought we could, but we really couldn't." Slowly and quietly they explained. As she heard the truth her attitude changed.

When the woman and her husband came to the arraignment that morning they had been determined to press charges, regardless of what happened. Now our attorney suggested that we offer her $100 to sign a statement that she would drop all charges. The fence was the only damage and it could be easily and quickly repaired. She agreed to that, and we were all released without having to go to trial.

The next day we called a news conference at the motel. The TV stations, radio stations and newspaper reporters all came. Rachel told her story and when she had finished, she and Janet fielded questions.

To me that was incredible. Sunday Rachel was deep in the cult. Monday she was grilled by police officers and made a court appearance. Tuesday morning she fielded the tough questions reporters asked.

That same day a man from Denver flew to St. Louis in his private plane to bring the Martins home. Rachel sat next to her mother. As the aircraft left the ground she looked out the window and saw that they were sitting over the wing. With tears welling in her soft brown eyes, she turned to her mother and told her of the talk she had had with one of the sisters about mounting up with wings as eagles and fleeing her enemies. She told of praying for deliverance when Jerry had come to get her, yet God had helped him and his friends.

"And, Mom," Rachel concluded, looking out the window at the plane's wings, "God gave me my wings."

17
Advice To Parents

KEN MARTIN

This has been Rachel's story, but it has been our story, too. Lillian and I are her parents. We took care of her as a baby, watched her grow and did what we could to raise her in the nurture and admonition of the Lord.

Her experience with the cult is past history. She is again the attractive, outgoing, bubbling girl she was before she accosted the brothers on the street that fateful night in Kearney, Nebraska. Her eyes have regained their sparkle and her dimples seem to deepen when she laughs. At times it is hard for us to realize that we actually did go through those agonizing months when we didn't know where she was or what she was doing.

Now that she is back it would be easy to rationalize what happened—to lay the responsibility on the vicious set of circumstances that were closing in on her from all sides until the only course she thought she had left was to run. But in honesty we know that we could not absolve ourselves of blame. We, too, are responsible.

We were aware of that, even before we got her back, and after she was home we began to search our hearts, asking ourselves the questions—hard questions that tore at us.

Rachel had been raised in a Christian home. We had seen to that. She knew Christ as her Saviour. We had been concerned about that, too. We saw that she attended a sound, Bible-believing and teaching church and Sunday school and had even enrolled her in a Christian high school as long as we were in Nebraska. She was sheltered from the world until she had had an opportunity to grow in her faith and develop convictions of her own. If any girl had every chance to become a mature, solid Christian, it was Rachel. Our other children were raised in the same environment with the same set of standards and guidance.

Why, then, did she go off the way she did, leaving everything she had been taught? Why did she renounce us and go with a group that demanded total subjection and a life of hardship and deprivation? Why did she allow herself to be burdened with laws and regulations so grievous to bear that no one in the cult was truly happy?

You will never know how many times we asked ourselves that question. Why? Why? WHY?

It would be easy for us to shift the responsibility to the school she attended in Denver. She was lonely there, and desperately anxious to be popular—so much so that her Christian standards were pushed aside. We could look at her stay in Kearney after her graduation, pointing the finger at her associates again, and calling attention to the fact that she was out from under the influence of the church and our Christian home for the first time, and was tempted to stray from the Lord.

If we do that, however, we would not be honest with ourselves, our daughter, or our God. And, equally important, we might give excuse to other parents to ignore their own shortcomings, their own sin, in dealing with their children. We might miss the opportunity to help them correct their faults and deal with potential problems before it is too late. We might miss the opportunity to encourage other Christian parents whose sons or daughters have gone off into cults and strange lifestyles. For those reasons we are going to be honest—as honest and soul-searching as we know how.

Some suggest that children—as they approach the bewildering, frustrating, difficult teens—be schooled in the precepts of the cults, so they are forewarned in case they come into contact with groups that might lead them astray. That might be practical in some instances, but there are more than 5,000 religious cults stalking our land. Some have as few as ten members. Others, like Transcendental Meditation, have 650,000 adherents and are adding new recruits at the rate of 1,500 each month.

The different groups are as varied in their teachings as the difference in the numbers of their following. Hare Krishnas, with their shaven heads (save for the ponytail or knot of hair to be used by the gods to lift them to heaven when they die), their saffron robes and chanting, have their roots in the mystic recesses of India. The Divine Light Mission recognizes all the religious bodies in the world, but modestly insists that they point to their own illustrious leader, Guru Maharaj Ji, who has been somewhat tarnished by unholy living and an unseemly struggle with his own mother—who first deified him and later rejected him.

There are others that have their beginnings in Christianity. The Church of Unification is one, with its emphasis on fund-raising and the infallibility of their leader, the Rev. Sun Myung Moon of Korea. They use the Bible but claim that both Adam and Jesus failed, leaving Rev. Moon as the Saviour of the world. The Bible is written in code, he teaches and he, alone, has the power to decode it. Lying, cheating and stealing mean nothing at all if they will promote the work of the church.

The Children of God also looks to Christianity as the seed of its origin. David Berg, the founder, was a minister at the time and professed to believe and preach salvation, but his own private interpretation of isolated verses and phrases provide a basis for gross immorality and any other excesses that come to his mind. Prospective members are threatened with impending doom if they don't make an immediate decision to join the group.

The People's Temple, so much in the news the latter part of 1978, was one of the larger cults. Like the Unification Church and the Children of God, their strength lay in their leader, Rev. Jim Jones. At first Jones only placed himself in a position equal with God. Later, when his followers were completely under his control, he dethroned Christ and made himself supreme. His goal: to set up a Communistic society for himself and his people.

Huge sums of money and hundreds of acres of valuable real estate were turned over to the Temple as new converts aligned themselves with the faithful. Eventually the holdings reached $15 million. Jones was a self-proclaimed minister with a degree in education, a master of manipulation who seemed to know, instinctively, the methods best suited to persuade his followers to do his bidding. And, when all else failed, he used drugs—or "drug therapy" as he liked to call it.

There are many similarities and differences between Jones and Jim Roberts, the leader of the group Rachel was with. Both were strong, charismatic personalities with the ability to attract large followings. Both used the Bible freely, pulling verses out of context to suit the purpose of the moment. Both claimed to have access to revelations direct from God, placing His blessings on their activities. Both encouraged their people to dispose of their worldly possessions and bring the proceeds to the "storehouse."

Yet, I must be fair. Roberts honestly believes that he is leading his people the way God would have them go. Jones was a cynic who stomped on the Bible in a rage because the people wanted to follow its dictates. Christianity was a sham to him, a cloak to make the communism he actually espoused palatable to his people. Roberts is just as wrong and has led his group just as far astray, but I am convinced that he is sincere.

Jones piled up a fortune of millions for himself and his church. There have been rumors that Roberts has done the same, but no one I have been able to talk to knows where such holdings are—if they do exist. Rachel tells of his using a portion of the money from the sale of her car to pay off her debts back in Kearney. Occasionally, when they were on the road, people would offer them money. If that happened, they accepted it, but they did not engage in fund raising efforts like most other cults.

Sex seemed to play a vital part in the People's Temple, with Jones taking any man or woman he wanted as a bed partner. The Roberts cult is puritanical by any standards. Girls could go off with any of the men for a week or a month without being molested or even propositioned. It was improper for a brother even to touch a sister's hand.

It was not until I heard Rachel being interviewed by the *Denver Post* at the contract signing for this book, however, that I realized exactly how sinister and evil the hold was that Brother Evangelist had on her and the others.

"Was suicide or murder ever discussed by your group?" the reporter asked.

She waited a moment, thinking. "No," she said, "it wasn't. Our group was non-violent. However, our minds were so thoroughly under Brother Evangelist's control that if he had asked us to take our own lives or murder someone, and we thought the whole group was going to do it, we would have."

If I had ever needed evidence that the group was not Christian, that was it.

Although the cults differ widely there are a few common denominators. In *Know The Marks Of The Cults* (Victor Books, 1975), Dave Breese lists them:

1. *Extra-Biblical revelation.* The placing of another document, often written by the founder or leader, alongside the Bible and claiming a special revelatory standing for it.
2. *A false basis of salvation.* Usually salvation by

works.

3. *Uncertain hope.*

4. *Presumptuous Messianic leadership.* The human leader is elevated to a messianic level.

5. *Doctrinal ambiguity.* The stress is commonly sub-rational, emotional, vaguely mystical, and without a clear or understandable basis.

6. *The claim of special discoveries.*

7. *Defective Christology.* The denying, in one way or another, of basic Biblical teachings concerning the nature and work of Christ.

8. *Segmented Biblical attention.* Picking and choosing a few verses or portions for emphasis that support or appear to support a particular teaching. The rest of the Bible is usually ignored.

9. *Enslaving organizational structure.* The creation of a monolithic, merciless, and entangling organizational structure. The loyalty appealed to is something other than Jesus Christ.

10. *Financial exploitation.*

11. *Denunciation of others.*

12. *Syncretism.* The supporting of a mishmash of ideas currently popular.

We have discovered another common denominator to add to the list above. Their prime recruiting grounds are college and university campuses and other areas where the young are to be found in large numbers.

It is always wise to educate your children in the teachings of the cults as much as you can. But don't neglect other, more important areas. Be sure that your children have been presented with the claims of Christ on their lives. It is not enough to see that they are in a sound, Bible-teaching Sunday school and church where they hear the teachings of God from the lips of dedicated men and women. Some young people go through their important, formative teens thinking they are Christians because they have believing parents and attend a good church. Such a boy or girl is like a tree without roots. Adversity, the first strong winds of opposition, or the tempting smile of some weird doctrine is often enough to shake his fragile faith. Sit down with your child and present Christ to him, step by step. Show him the importance *you* place on a personal relationship with Jesus Christ.

Dr. Theodore Epp, founder of Back to the Bible Broadcast, gave a friend of ours a formula for leading his children to Christ:

1. Let him hear the plan of salvation from your lips.
2. Live a consistent Christian life before him.
3. See that he attends Sunday school and church where the Bible is taught as the true Word of God.
4. Pray for him without ceasing.

How I have thanked God that we did not fail Rachel in those areas. Our mistakes were legion, but we were not deficient in presenting Christ to her as practically and as consistently as possible, both in words and in our own lives. And we saw that she had sound teaching through the church. But, somehow, in our efforts to make sure that she lived a life of separation from the things of the world, we gave her the impression that being a Christian was a matter of legality, of keeping a list of rules and observing certain obligations.

We said that we believed in salvation by faith, not works—but we stressed our list of do's and don'ts so much that in her eyes they became the cornerstone of our Christianity. She saw salvation as a heavy burden, the keeping of a set of standards she did not subscribe to, of regulations forced on her by her mother and me, who must not have wanted her to have any fun.

We were happy in Christ ourselves, but were so busy I don't think we realized her need for wholesome fun and the vitality of a vibrant Christian life. We didn't see the importance of playing together and demonstrating to her the real joy there is in walking with God.

During the time Rachel was with the cult we realized that one of the stronger appeals such groups make is to kids who are dissatisfied and disillusioned with their old lives. Rachel had seen the world as more appealing than the Christian life as she saw it being lived around her. She had thought she was missing something by living for God, and began the double standards that soon took hold of her life. Too late she realized that it ended in such bitterness and unhappiness, and the cult of Brother Evangelist seemed the only way out. She felt a life of complete devotion and subjection was all that could atone for her sin.

We also failed in keeping the lines of communication open. That is much easier to talk about than it is to do. There is a natural reluctance on the part of some teenagers to share anything with their parents. There is the feeling that their mother and father somehow were able to reach their present stage in life without learning anything.

The easy thing when one is confronted with that situation is to throw up one's hands in despair and quit trying. We have to learn to understand these bewildering, often infuriating teenaged children of ours, caught up as they are in that never-never land where they are neither children nor adults, where they resent discipline yet long for controls to set the limits of their conduct.

The barriers between ourselves and our children exist and have to be broken down if we are to communicate with them successfully. We must acknowledge that at the very beginning. And, we are the ones who are going to have to get rid of those barriers. Our children, unless they are different from most, will retreat behind a wall of resentment and frustration, resigning themselves to the fact that nobody understands them. They may reach out toward us, clumsily, as Rachel did when she came to Denver just to talk to us a short time before going off with the cult and wound up writing a note that we should have recognized as a desperate cry for help. But our kids are so confused and bewildered by all the problems of growing into adulthood that their efforts to communicate with us are going to be hesitant and feeble, at best. We are the ones who have to bridge the gap. And why shouldn't it be that way? We are the ones who have walked the road between childhood and maturity and should know the conflicting emotions and problems it causes.

But how?

Some parents try by acting like teenagers themselves, by trying to get down on the level of their children. Kids have shown that they don't want that. I remember one girl who complained that her mother's giddy actions and too-young clothes made her jealous. She had the uneasy feeling that her mom was after her boyfriend. The truth was that he bored her mother silly. Communicating with your teenager doesn't mean that. Besides, what thirty-five or forty-year-old can act like he's sixteen and not make a fool of himself? Parents should not attempt to make themselves "best buddies" with their kids. Our sons and daughters still want us to be Mother and Dad. They like the relationship and need it. Fortunately, we can communicate best with them on that basis.

First, we must spend time with our kids in some sort of activity that is enjoyable for both them and us. Rachel used to enjoy hanging around the print shop with me. Looking back, I wish I had asked her to help. I could have found something for her to do and we could have chatted while we worked. That could have done much to break down her hesitance in sharing her problems with me.

Second, I should have been less critical of her, her friends and her opinions. That is difficult for a parent to refrain from. Ever since our children were born we have been charged with the responsibility of guiding, training and disciplining them. It is difficult to shove those things on the back burner, even for a little while. However, if I could turn the clock back I would take a lesson from a successful grandparent I know. He spends time with his grandchildren on a warm, personal basis. He doesn't scold or advise unless it is imperative. The kids love to be with him and never seem to tire of talking to him and sharing their problems. I would spend more time with Rachel, if I could live those formative years over. I would put my own desire to correct and chastise aside for a time and allow her to get acquainted with me as a person.

If I embarrassed or offended her I would apologize and ask her forgiveness and, above all, I would be honest with her. I would let her see my humanness and frailties—not by confessions, but simply by acknowledging through my actions that I know my own weaknesses and often fail. I would also show her that I go to Christ, asking His forgiveness for my sin.

I would try to plan more things that would cause her to want to be with us. This isn't easy with a teenager. All their lives they have wanted to be out from under our direction. It is only natural that they would want to begin going with their own friends and doing things that the gang wants to do.

While it may sound like a contradiction, I would retain and practice the right to know who she was with, where she was going and what time she would be home. Teenagers are inexperienced in this area and need our guidance. I would let her know I was concerned about those things because I loved her, but I would still insist that I know, and that she follow my direction for as long as she lived at home or was being supported at school.

The cults do some of their most serious recruiting just before and just after final exams on college campuses. The kids are exhausted from study and emotionally drained. Depression and frustration builds. It is at such times that your youngster is more subject to the siren call of the Moonies or the Hare Krishnas, or one of the others.

If you wish to help your child resist the efforts of the cults to enlist him, be particularly concerned about those natural times of frustration and depression. Phone and write frequently, or if possible, make occasion to visit—anything that would help lend stability and strength to your child's resolve.

Be sensitive to the moods of his letters and phone calls. Most of us signal our need for help in a variety of ways. If your youngster is like Rachel, he will signal his need as well. Watch prayerfully for any change in his attitude or emotional stability. Losing a job, being laid off work, financial problems, failing a subject, or breaking up with a girl or boyfriend can all be upsetting experiences. Be alert to those times of special need in your youngster's life and give him extra encouragement and love to help get him back on track again. Remember, those opportunities can either help you and your child to draw closer together, or will cause you to draw farther apart. They might even be a means for Satan to get his claws on your child through one of the cults.

Finally, if I could turn the clock back, I would go to far greater efforts to show her that I loved her, that no matter what happened or what she did, we still loved her and were solidly behind her. Many teens get the impression that their parents don't love them—a factor that can cause more trouble than the average youngster would admit.

If we had done all those things to the best of our ability, I admit that she could still have gone off with the cult of Brother Evangelist. Even if we had done everything exactly the way a parent should—showed her our love, did all sorts of things with her, and spent time with her without overbearing criticism or correction, I would accept the fact that she was a free moral agent and that she might very well go off with a group.

However, I would not change a single thing we did in our efforts to get her back. We did not lose faith that God would one day bring about her release from the cult. And I would advise other parents to do the same. Having

Rachel go off with the group was the most traumatic experience Lillian and I have ever gone through. Yet, we learned anew that God is faithful and that all things work together for good for those who put their trust in Him.

What should you do if, in spite of all your teaching and concern and teaching of your church, your child turns on you and goes off with one of the many cults?

1. *Don't waste valuable time and emotional energy in self-recrimination.* If you feel at fault, ask God to forgive you and get on with the task of locating your youngster and getting him back.

2. *Study the cults.* Your library should have a host of books on the cults. Learn as much as you can about them and study their methods of recruiting, teaching and fund raising. The more you learn about them the more likely you are to be successful in your search and in getting your child released.

Although there are certain similarities in all the cults, your task will be simpler if you know which one your son or daughter is with. It will narrow your field of study.

Seek out the kids who have been in the various cults and have been released and deprogrammed. They can give you invaluable first-hand information. They can tell you how the group travels, and the cities or areas they prefer. We learned, for example, that the group Rachel was in had certain places they visited from time to time—places where they had made friends with the local police or where they had found it easier to get by, for one reason or another. Learn who the leaders are, as much of their doctrine and rules as you can, and any problems the group has.

3. *Contact the parents of other kids in the cult and keep in touch with them.* Exchange information with them. It was through the parents of the girl in the Denver area that we first learned of her deprogramming. She furnished the tip that the group was in St. Louis, and that tip led to Rachel's rescue.

4. *Contact the parents of kids who have left the particular group your son or daughter is in.* They can help you to get to know and understand more about the group.

5. *Get in touch with groups engaged in helping parents locate their children, getting them out of the cults, and deprogramming them.* Arrange for the help of those you know to be reputable, if you are financially able to do so. They can help you with the legal elements involved. The situation is constantly changing. What we were able to do with Rachel might mean serious trouble for you today.

In enlisting the aid of outsiders, use the utmost care in checking out anyone before you confide in them or give them money. We, and several other parents I know, were completely taken in by one young man who professed, among other things, to be a Christian. He stole from us and obtained money under false pretenses. A reputable individual or organization in this field will not hesitate to give references. Be sure to check on them.

6. *Don't be disturbed about putting your child through deprogramming.* It is not the horror it has been described as being. In the case of Bruce Surber, a twenty-three-year-old former medical student who was taken from Brother Evangelist's group in Tucson in the fall of 1975, the judge placed him in the custody of his wife. Dr. Kenneth Gilmartin, a clinical psychologist, testified at his hearing that he was unable to make decisions for himself.

"His thinking is disturbed," Dr. Gilmartin said. "He doesn't deal in the realm of reality. His ability to make lucid decisions is nonexistent at this time. Brainwashing is definitely involved."

He described the process of recruitment as having three phases:

Isolation. New recruits are allowed no contact with anyone but group members and no external stimulation. New members always are accompanied by old ones and their access to outside news is controlled.

Thought control. With irregular hours of sleeping and eating, new recruits are given a black-and-white yardstick for good and evil after confessing past sins and expressing guilt for them.

Platitude conditioning. Conditioned responses, usually memorized Biblical quotations, are given to all questions.

Eugene Wyman, who has made an extensive study of cults and their methods, adds several other factors that are used in educating and conditioning a new recruit:

Tenseness.

A fear-love relationship.

Repetition.

Disguised threats.

Gilmartin summed up the process by saying, "A typical pattern of indoctrination used by the group consisted of isolating new members from all contact with the outside world, establishing a rigid new value system for them and forcing them to memorize religious response to any situation or question."

Nikki Barker, who lived in our home for a time following her rescue from the group, has assisted several parents in the deprogramming of their children. "Deprogramming is *not* a forcible change, nor is it another form of mind control, as some would have you believe," Nikki says. "It is simply getting the individual to the place where he is once again able to think for himself and to make his own decisions regarding his religious and physical needs.

"You try to get an emotional response, so that you have more than a zombie reaction from the person. You want to make the person start thinking for himself, not just in terms of what the group has taught. If one has been brainwashed, he does not have a free will.

"Fortunately, I just snapped out of it," she continued, speaking of her own shedding of the shackles of psychological imprisonment. "Like the sun had broken through a bunch of clouds. All of a sudden the clouds were gone. But others need to be helped."

When your son or daughter is being deprogrammed, he will have to be confined. He will have been taught to resist the "evil deprogrammers" and try to escape. So he will try every means possible to get away. It has taken time to get him into this condition and it takes time to get him out. This also explains why deprogramming is done in seclusion, with the least possible commotion, and with few people involved.

There are cases where kids have escaped before being deprogrammed and have sued their parents for interfering with their religious freedom. Yet there is no freedom in the cults. The convert is often required to bring in money through the sale of flowers, candy, etc. Hare Krishna requires a certain amount of time proselytizing travelers and selling or distributing literature in airports. Another group demands that their people bring in a certain amount of money or distribute a given amount of literature. In the group Rachel was with, such things as taking baths and using the bathroom were taken as fleshly desires to be conquered. And everything the sisters did was done only after obtaining permission from the brothers.

7. Once your child is out of the cult, you must do something to fill the void in his life. He joined the group because of a need he felt was not being met. When the cult teachings are then removed, the void must be filled. In Rachel's case, with her background in the Bible and being able to throw her questions at Jerry and get straight, Bible-based answers, it was quite natural for Jesus to fill that void.

We have had the privilege of counseling a number of young men and women who have come out of the cults. We encourage them to get involved in a sound, Bible-teaching and believing church. Those who were Christians before going into the cult seem to have less difficulty adjusting to a normal Christian life afterward. For those who are unbelievers, the deprogramming is only the beginning. We have urged them to get involved with believers in a church situation and have prayed for them often, but that is about all we have been able to do for them.

Finally, I would plead with you to remember in prayer all of these kids, into whichever cult they have been lured. They are sincere in what they are doing, and are incapable of thinking things out for themselves. Pray that God might be able to speak to them through the inconsistencies of the group the way He was able to speak to Rachel. Pray for those who are still in, that in one way or another they might be gotten out and deprogrammed. Many dear friends of Rachel's are still captives of the group, bound by a fiendish legalism.

And don't neglect to pray for those who have gotten out, that they will replace their loyalty to the cult with a strong loyalty to Jesus Christ. There is a floating period for those who have been deprogrammed. During that time they might go back if approached by other members.

If we were to choose the one thing that held us together as a family and kept Lillian and me going during the nineteen months Rachel was away, it would be prayer. The power of prayer is wonderful and powerful beyond human comprehension. Pray for your children as they go through the difficult teen years, asking God to strengthen their faith and to keep them from the false teachings that abound. And pray for your child if he succumbs to the siren song and goes off into a cult. Above all, pray and never give up hope.

18
Since My Rescue

RACHEL

When I was taken out of the cult in March, 1977, I at first struggled with sharing my testimony personally. For a while I was being asked every day to go somewhere and speak, when all I wanted to do was get on with my life. I became very tired and almost bitter toward people for asking me to tell the story again and again. I didn't want to talk about my experience. Instead, I wanted to go to a secluded spot where I could rest and learn about the Lord.

I didn't realize that I was growing through it all. I was learning to lean on the Lord when I didn't feel I could speak again. I was also learning to say "No, I'm sorry, but I can't come now." That, too, was hard for me.

That was the situation when I went back to school—at Western Bible College, where my dad works—eager to learn. I wasn't even thinking of dating until I met Dennis Dugger there. Our friendship grew very close, and Dennis helped me tremendously by listening to me and encouraging me. He is now my loving husband, and I'm so thankful for him. Being married and having a home of my own has played a big part in helping me become myself again.

I have come a long way since my stay with the Jim Roberts group. I'm thankful for the restored relationships with the Lord and with my parents. I worked in

Dad's print shop for awhile and things have been really great between us. My folks are wonderful people.

Just recently I began a new job as a nurse's aide at a nursing home. I plan to enter LPN training soon to become a licensed practical nurse, and Dennis and I are looking toward possible work on the mission field.

So my life has settled down, and I am relaxed again. I have a new desire to serve God—He has recently opened more opportunities for me to share my story with others. And I can see how my story in print can be used by Him to help so many more people than those I can talk to personally.

I was able to help two girls who had been in a group called "The Forever Family" and had just been deprogrammed. Hearing of my experiences seemed to help them get their thinking together.

Also, a boy came out to Denver from North Platte to talk with me. He was about to join a cult that sounded just like Jim Roberts' group. He had been so taken in by the group that he had already given two of the men $1100 from his savings. When his parents discovered what was happening, they called a Christian psychology instructor at Kearney State College, and since he knew of my experiences, he phoned to see if I would help.

The boy agreed to come to Denver to talk with me, but he told his parents, "That girl doesn't know what I'm going through. There's nothing she can say that will change my mind."

As we talked, his experience was so similar to mine that I could hardly believe it. The things he told me about meeting the men and what they said and how he felt—*I knew what it was like!* His coming out here to talk to me and a deprogrammer saved him and his parents a lot of misery. He is so thankful now that he did not join that cult.

One day a lady from Connecticut phoned me. Her daughter had joined the Jim Roberts cult in June, 1978, and her mother needed the encouragement of knowing that it is possible for a member to be brought out of the group.

I felt so sorry for her. She kept asking simple questions about how we lived, where we slept, and what we ate. We talked and talked and talked, although we were on long distance. As we hung up, I thought, "Oh, if I could just send her my book—my testimony in detail—so she could know what I went through."

My prayer is that this book will be a source of encouragement and practical help to parents and loved ones of any young people who might be susceptible to the lure of the cults. And, most of all, I hope it will help educate and dissuade those young persons who may someday be enticed by a cult member or leader.

I have seen again and again recently how relevant the story is. The cults are still alive and going strong, and young people are still being lured into them, just as I was. And now that my mind is cleared, I want to be more available for the Lord to use for His glory. If I can help steer one young person away from the cults, then my experience will not have been in vain.

Rachel Martin Dugger—today.